MONEY'S

GUIDE

TO SECURE

INVESTING

Written by

Jordan E. Goodman and the

Editors of MONEY Magazine

Contents

[INTRO]

MONEY'S Guide to Secure Investing **p a g e 5**

[ONE]

Cash Instruments **p a g e 7**

[TWO]

Investing in Stocks **p a g e 1 8**

[THREE]

Selecting the Best Mutual Funds **p a g e 4 3**

[FOUR]

Investing in Bonds **p a g e 6 0**

[FIVE]

Speculating with Futures and Options **p a g e 1 0 2**

[SIX]

Other Investments: Gold, Real Estate **p a g e 1 0 9**

[SEVEN]

Investment Strategies for Every Age Category **p a g e 1 2 3**

[INTRO]

Money's Guide to Secure Investing

While you probably spend most of your time and effort earning money by working at your job, you most likely pay too little attention to how to invest your money wisely. *Money's Guide to Secure Investing* will provide the basic information you need to make your money work as hard for you as you do to earn it.

You must take two actions to turn into a smart investor: Become knowledgeable about your investment options, and establish habits to set aside money so you can put your knowledge into action. This *Guide* will explain the pros and cons of the many investment choices you have today. In addition, we recommend that you read Money Magazine every month in order to follow the relative attractiveness of each of the options presented in this *Guide*, which will change based on changes in the economy, interest rates, securities prices and world events.

Establishing the investing habit is up to you. No one will do it for you. Whatever it takes – whether it be setting up an automatic investing program with your employer or a mutual fund, or remembering to pay yourself first each time you get a paycheck – you must get in the habit of putting aside funds that will otherwise surely be spent. If you do not establish such a habit, you will not accumulate the capital you need to fund your most important life goals, such as a down payment on a house, a college education for your children or your comfortable retirement.

This *Guide* is divided into seven easy-to-read sections. We explain cash instruments, stocks, stock mutual funds, bonds and bond mutual funds, futures and options, and gold, other precious metals and investment real estate. In the final section, we offer some advice on investing based on your age: We discuss strategies for those in their 20s and 30s, 40s and 50s, and in the retired years of 60 and up. The *Guide* is packed with easy-to-use worksheets, clear illustrations and specific examples that should help you understand each of the main areas of investing.

The material in this *Guide* has been adapted from *Everyone's Money Book*, written by MONEY Magazine's Wall Street Correspondent, Jordan E. Goodman. We hope you enjoy your *Guide to Secure Investing*. If you put into action the enhanced understanding of investments you gain from the *Guide*, you should be able to meet your lifetime financial goals!

[ONE]

Cash Instruments

ash instruments play an important stabilizing role in your investment portfolio. No matter how much or how little your cash earns for you in interest, it cannot fall in principal value, which certainly cannot be said for stocks and bonds. Cash can therefore act as a haven when stock and bond prices are falling.

Clearly, it is important to have cash available to meet everyday living expenses. Many cash instruments, including money-market accounts, NOW accounts, and passbook savings accounts, are instantly accessible either through a check privilege or by withdrawing cash at an automatic teller machine (ATM). Other cash vehicles, including CDs and T-bills, which have short maturities, allow you to get at your money when the instruments mature in a few months. The liquidity of cash is one of its main benefits.

[Types of Cash Instruments]

In deciding how much money to allocate to the different kinds of cash accounts, you should consider both convenience and yield. Because all of these alternatives are absolutely safe, they belong on the bottom, or low-risk level, of your investment pyramid (see Figure 1 on next page).What follows is a rundown of the advantages and disadvantages of the different kinds of cash instruments, starting with the lowest yielding and running through the highest yielding.

NOW and Super-NOW Checking Accounts

Before the mid-1970s, checking accounts paid no interest. The introduction of the money-market mutual fund forced banks to respond by offering what was called a *negotiable order of withdrawal* (NOW) account. At first, these accounts

Fig. ① Investment Risk Levels

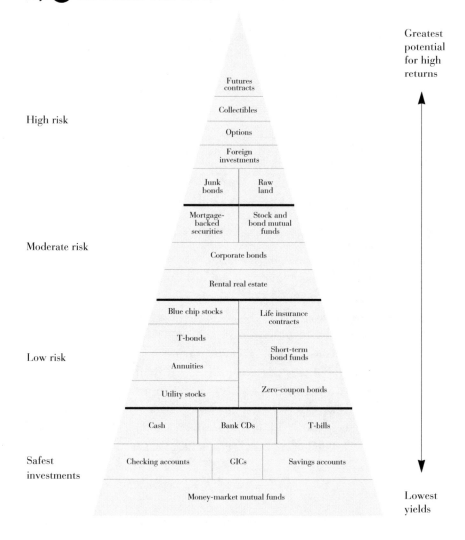

Greatest potential for high returns

High risk

- Futures contracts
- Collectibles
- Options
- Foreign investments
- Junk bonds | Raw land
- Mortgage-backed securities | Stock and bond mutual funds

Moderate risk

- Corporate bonds
- Rental real estate

- Blue chip stocks | Life insurance contracts
- T-bonds
- Annuities | Short-term bond funds
- Utility stocks | Zero-coupon bonds

Low risk

- Cash | Bank CDs | T-bills

Safest investments

- Checking accounts | GICs | Savings accounts
- Money-market mutual funds

Lowest yields

could pay a maximum of 5.25 percent interest, but by the mid-1980s, banks were free to pay whatever they chose. Rates rose a bit higher but then fell to the 2 percent-to-3 percent range by the early 1990s.

NOW and super-NOW accounts allow unlimited writing of checks of any size. In return, banks often require minimum balances of at least $1,000, and they charge service fees if you do not keep enough money in the account. Some banks will also charge for every check you write if you do not maintain the minimum balance. Before you sign up for a NOW account, see whether you typically keep enough in your checking account to earn more in interest than you will pay in fees.

Passbook Savings Accounts

Long the staple of bank depositors, the passbook savings account is not as popular as it used to be. In the 1970s, it was about the only account a bank offered that paid interest – usually 5.25 percent – and that provided instant access to your money. The bank provided a passbook in which it would post your interest and balances.

These days, passbook accounts often don't even come with passbooks. Because you can put money into them or take money out whenever you want, they are called *day-to-day savings accounts*. Instead of receiving a passbook, you get a monthly statement from the bank updating your balance and the amount of interest earned.

Unless you do not have enough money to meet minimum balance requirements on other higher yielding accounts, passbook savings plans are not very attractive investments. The fees a bank charges to maintain a passbook account may eat up a significant portion of your interest earnings unless you maintain a large enough balance.

Money-Market Deposit Accounts

Money-market deposit accounts (MMDAs) are the banking industry's answer to the money-market mutual fund. They were first offered as banking was deregulated in the early 1980s to allow banks to compete against the money funds that were attracting billions of dollars in deposits.

Banks can pay whatever they wish on MMDAs. Their rates will always be higher than those on NOW or passbook savings accounts, though not always much higher. In the early days of deregulation, banks paid hefty double-digit rates, but by the early 1990s, MMDA yields had plunged to about 3 percent to 4 percent. Bankers will usually adjust their MMDA rates on a weekly basis, based on what competing banks and money-market mutual funds are offering and what is happening to the general direction of interest rates, particularly short-term rates such as Treasury bills. Because MMDAs track the general direction of interest rates, you will benefit if yields rise sharply. However, this is a short-term rate, and you cannot lock in a high yield unless you convert to some form of fixed-income security, such as a bond or a long-term CD.

Unlike your access to a NOW account, your access to an MMDA is somewhat restricted. According to federal banking law, you can write three checks of any amount and make three electronic transfers a month on your MMDA. Those electronic transfers might be made by telephone, at an automatic teller machine or as an automatic payment to a third party, like a utility. Your best strategy is to make three large transfers a month into your checking account, for which you can write checks. This way, most of your money will be earning high interest for a longer period of time.

As they do for other accounts, banks usually require a minimum balance of at least $1,000 to open an MMDA. Most banks also charge fees for keeping a low balance, though often they will pay higher interest if you keep more money in your account.

If you want to consolidate most of your cash at a bank in one liquid account, the MMDA is the best place to do it. It will pay the highest yields of any readily accessible product the bank offers.

Money-Market Mutual Funds

Though many people think money-market mutual funds are the same as MMDAs, there are several important differences between them:

Money-market mutual funds are run by fund management companies, and they buy short-term securities that offer the best yields available in the marketplace at that time. The money funds buy high-quality, short-term obligations called commercial paper, banker's acceptances, CDs, repurchase agreements, and Treasury bills, and they pass on all of their income, minus management fees, to shareholders in the funds. In contrast, bank MMDA funds are not invested in the money markets directly. They are lent by the bank to corporations and consumers, and the bank keeps whatever difference there is between the loan proceeds and the money-market yield.

Unlike bank MMDAs, money-market mutual funds are not insured by the FDIC or any other government agency. Though there has never been a default or even a near-default in a money-market mutual fund, there is usually no insurance company guaranteeing that it will cover losses in the unlikely case of such a default. (A few money funds do carry such insurance.) Ultimately, the fund management company stands behind the guarantee that you will be able to withdraw your money from a money fund. In a few cases where there were temporary problems with a money fund, the fund company immediately bailed out shareholders. One advantage of having assets in a money fund that is part of a larger mutual fund family is that you can transfer money into or out of the money fund with a simple toll-free phone call.

Money-market mutual funds have a net asset value that is kept stable at $1 a share, while there is no price per share set for bank MMDAs. Money funds set up the $1-a-share system when they were introduced in the mid-1970s, and allowing people to know that the number of shares they own is exactly equal to the dollar value of their accounts has worked well. In the money fund business, it would be considered a violation of the worst kind to "break the buck," or $1 share price, for any reason.

Money-market mutual funds assess annual management fees of less than 1 percent annually, which is deducted automatically from a fund's yield. The industry average is .75 percent, and any fee over 1 percent is excessive. So if the fund earned an 8 percent yield last year and it levies a 1 percent management fee, you will earn 7 percent. Sometimes, if money funds get into a war for business, they will waive some or all of their management fees for a few months, which will instantly raise the funds' yields. In contrast, banks do not charge management fees. Instead, they impose minimum balance requirements and service fees.

Money-market mutual funds usually impose a minimum amount on checks that ranges from $100 to $500, while bank MMDAs usually allow checks of any amount. All brokerage asset management accounts come with money-market funds on which you can write checks.

Money-market mutual funds come in both taxable and tax-free varieties, while interest from bank MMDAs is always taxable. Money-market funds offer three *taxable* varieties: Treasury-only, government-only, and general-purpose. Treasury-only funds buy exclusively Treasury bills and other direct obligations of the U.S. government. These are the safest, but lowest-yielding, money funds. The government-only funds invest solely in paper that is backed either directly or indirectly by the government. These funds are extremely safe, yet they pay slightly higher yields than Treasury funds. General-purpose money funds buy obligations of both domestic and foreign governments and corporations. While these are also very safe, there is a bit more risk that a corporate issuer will default. As a result, these money-market funds pay the highest yields, which may be as much as a percentage point higher than government funds. Whether you opt for a government or a general-purpose fund depends on your tolerance for risk, though a general-purpose money-market fund should hardly be considered a trip to the roulette wheel.

Money-market mutual funds are also available in *tax-free* form. These funds buy the short-term debt of states and municipalities and pass all their income, minus management fees, to shareholders. There are hundreds of national tax-exempt funds to choose from, either directly from fund companies or indirectly through brokerage firm asset management accounts. The percentage yield on these funds will always be lower than that of taxable money-market funds, but if your tax bracket is high enough, you will have more money in your pocket after taxes with a tax-exempt money fund. In some high-tax cities like New York, there are even triple-tax-exempt money funds, which buy only debt of the city. Shareholders in these funds thereby avoid federal, state, and city income taxes. For you to determine whether it makes more sense to keep cash in a taxable or a tax-free money fund, perform the following calculation, called *finding the taxable equivalent yield of your money fund.* It is the same method you would use when considering buying a municipal bond.

Deduct your federal tax bracket percentage from 100. In this example, we will use a 31 percent tax bracket. The result is known as the reciprocal of your tax bracket.

> 100 − 31 Tax bracket = 69 Reciprocal of tax bracket

Divide the tax-free yield on the money fund you are considering by the reciprocal of your tax bracket. In this case, we will assume that your tax-free money fund pays a 5 percent tax-free yield.

> $$\frac{5\% \text{ Tax-free money-fund yield}}{69 \text{ Reciprocal of tax bracket}} = 7.25\% \text{ Taxable equivalent yield}$$

This means that you would have to find a taxable money fund paying 7.25 percent to end up with the same dollars in your pocket after taxes that the 5 percent tax-free will pay you.

To determine whether a double-tax-free or triple-tax-free money fund makes sense, go through the same exercise, adding in your state and local tax brackets. If your combined federal, state and local tax brackets add up to 40 percent, for example, the taxable equivalent yield of a 5 percent triple-tax-free money fund would be an astounding 8.33 percent!

> $$\frac{5\% \text{ Tax-free money-fund yield}}{60 \text{ Reciprocal of tax bracket}} = 8.33\% \text{ Taxable equivalent yield}$$

Now you can see why tax-free money funds are so popular. Like taxable money funds, tax-free money funds permit you to write checks, usually with a minimum size of at least $100.

Money-market mutual fund yields are usually higher than those paid by bank MMDAs. Fund managers have a certain amount of flexibility in managing their funds that allows them to maximize yields. Money-market mutual funds, by law, cannot buy securities with maturities of longer than one year, and the average maturity of their entire portfolio cannot exceed 90 days. The longer the maturity of the paper they hold, the higher the funds' yields, and the longer those yields will last.

Fund managers who anticipate falling interest rates will lengthen the maturity of their holdings to be able to hang on to high yields for as long as possible. On the other hand, if managers think rates will rise, they will shorten the maturity of their holdings so they mature quickly, allowing them to buy more debt securities as soon as the yields are higher. The average maturity of all mutual funds is published every week in *The Wall Street Journal* and other financial newspapers, so you can tell whether maturities in the industry in general, and in any particular fund, are lengthening or shortening. Because of the different maturities of money funds, their yields tend to lag behind the movement in overall short-term rates. That is an advantage when rates are falling because you will be earning a high yield for a longer time. But when rates shoot up sharply, money fund yields take a while to catch up.

Money-market mutual funds are widely diversified. Securities and Exchange Commission (SEC) regulations prohibit money funds from investing more than 5 percent of their assets in the paper of a single company, or any more than 25 percent in one industry. In addition, SEC rules force money funds to buy commercial paper that is in either of the top two quality ratings – A1 or A2 by Standard & Poor's, or P1 or P2 by Moody's Investors Service. In contrast, all of your money is with one bank if it is in a bank MMDA, though if the funds are insured, there is nothing to worry about.

Money-market funds are credited with interest daily, and the interest is reinvested automatically in more fund shares. Banks can pay interest on MMDAs daily, weekly, or monthly. When it is credited to your account, interest also compounds automatically.

Treasury Bills

T-bills, as they are called, provide the ultimate in safety and liquidity and are therefore among investors' favorite havens for cash. Treasury bills are backed by the full faith and credit of the U.S. government, so for all practical purposes, they carry no risk of default.

Any Treasury security that is issued with a maturity of one year or less is called a Treasury bill. They are normally auctioned to the public every Monday in three-month and six-month maturities. (The Treasury calls them 13-week and 26-week bills). Once a month, the Treasury sells one-year (or 52-week) bills. Normally, the longer you commit your money, the higher your yield will be. Yields on Treasury bills tend to be lower than yields on money-market mutual funds because of the extra security that T-bills offer.

You can buy a Treasury bill directly from any Federal Reserve Bank or branch, either in person or by mail, with no fee. You can also write or visit the Bureau of Public Debt at the Treasury Department (Washington, DC 20239). You must fill out a form called a *tender* (see Figure 2), which means that you are making what is known as a *noncompetitive bid*, and submit a check for at least $10,000, the minimum accepted for a Treasury bill purchase. By submitting this bid, you are agreeing to accept whatever yield emerges from the Treasury auction

Fig. **2** Tender for 13-Week Treasury Bill

FORM PD F 5176-1
(February 1990)

OMB No. 1535-0069
Expires: 09-30-92

TENDER FOR 13-WEEK TREASURY BILL

TENDER INFORMATION

AMOUNT OF TENDER: $ _____

FOR DEPARTMENT USE

BID TYPE (Check One) ☐ NONCOMPETITIVE ☐ COMPETITIVE AT __ . __ %

ACCOUNT NUMBER

__ - __ - __

TENDER NUMBER
912794

INVESTOR INFORMATION

ACCOUNT NAME

CUSIP

ISSUE DATE

RECEIVED BY

DATE RECEIVED

ADDRESS

EXT REG ☐
FOREIGN ☐
BACKUP ☐
REVIEW ☐

CITY   STATE   ZIP CODE

TAXPAYER IDENTIFICATION NUMBER

1ST NAMED OWNER __ - __ - __   **OR**   __ - __

CLASS ☐

SOCIAL SECURITY NUMBER   EMPLOYER IDENTIFICATION NUMBER

TELEPHONE NUMBERS

WORK (__) __ - __   HOME (__) __ - __

PAYMENT ATTACHED

TOTAL PAYMENT: $ _____

NUMBERS

CASH (01): $ _____   CHECKS (02/03): $ _____

SECURITIES (05): $ _____ $ _____

OTHER (06): $ _____ $ _____

DIRECT DEPOSIT INFORMATION

ROUTING NUMBER

FINANCIAL INSTITUTION NAME

ACCOUNT NUMBER

ACCOUNT NAME

·ACCOUNT TYPE
(Check One)
☐ CHECKING
☐ SAVINGS

AUTOMATIC REINVESTMENT

1 2 3 4 5 6 7 8   Circle the number of sequential 13-week reinvestments you want to schedule at this time

AUTHORIZATION

For the notice required under the Privacy and Paperwork Reduction Acts, see the accompanying instructions.

I submit this tender pursuant to the provisions of Department of the Treasury Circulars, Public Debt Series Nos. 1-86 and 2-86 and the public announcement issued by the Department of the Treasury.

Under penalties of perjury, I certify that the number shown on this form is my correct taxpayer identification number and that I am not subject to backup withholding because (1) I have not been notified that I am subject to backup withholding as a result of a failure to report all interest or dividends, or (2) the Internal Revenue Service has notified me that I am no longer subject to backup withholding. I further certify that all other information provided on this form is true, correct and complete.

_____   _____
SIGNATURE   DATE

SEE INSTRUCTIONS FOR PRIVACY ACT AND PAPERWORK REDUCTION ACT NOTICE

★U.S.GPO:1990-268-403/20484

at which you are bidding. Professional government securities traders submit competitive bids for millions of dollars of bills. The supply of and demand for bills ultimately determine the average yield on each T-bill auction.

Alternatively, you can buy a Treasury bill through any broker or bank for a minimal charge of about $25. That fee, of course, reduces your effective yield. Once you have bought a T-bill, your name will be kept in the Treasury's electronic records. Don't expect a fancy certificate to be sent to you.

The investment yield method.

Once the yield on the T-bill has been set by the auction, which will be determined before 2 PM of that day and reported in newspapers the next day, the Treasury will immediately send you a refund check for what is known as the *discount*. The discount is the difference between $10,000 and the market price of the T-bill at that point. For example, if the auction produces a yield of 5.26 percent, you will receive a check for a discount of $500, which represents your return on investment. Your $9,500 remains with the Treasury until the bill matures. To calculate your yield for a one-year T-bill, divide the discount by the effective purchase price, which is $10,000 minus $500 in this case:

$$\$500 \text{ Discount} \div \$9,500 \text{ Effective purchase price} = 5.26\% \text{ Investment yield}$$

For a three- or six-month T-bill, you have to annualize the yield. For a three-month T-bill, you multiply the yield (5.26%) by 365, then divide by 91. For a six-month T-bill, you multiply the yield by 365, then divide by 182 as follows:

$$\frac{\$500 \text{ Discount}}{\$9,500 \text{ Effective purchase price}} \times \frac{365}{182} = 10.5\% \text{ Investment yield}$$

This yield is also known as the coupon-equivalent yield because it is measuring your return on the principal you have tied up in the T-bill until maturity. When the T-bill matures in three or six months, you receive a check for $10,000.

Like the interest on all Treasury securities, your T-bill's interest is taxable for federal income tax purposes, but it is not taxable at the state or local level. This gives a boost to the after-tax return you earn from the T-bill, particularly if you live in a high-tax state like New York or California. Taxes are due in the year the T-bill matures or is sold; therefore, if you want to delay taxes into the next year, you can buy a T-bill that matures after the next January 1.

If you need to cash in your T-bill before maturity, you can sell it but may not receive the best price. However, if interest rates have risen between the time you bought it and when you want to sell it, the T-bill's price will have dropped.

The yield is the coupon-equivalent yield. That is, it is based on your return on the capital you have tied up in the T-bill until maturity. In the first case here, the yield is 2.99 percent. It would be calculated as follows:

$291 Discount ÷ $9,709 Remaining principal = 5.2% Investment yield

This means that you would have $9,709 tied up until the T-bill matures, when you would receive a check from the Treasury for $10,000. Your interest would be $291.

Treasury bills might be right for you if you want total security and liquidity and you have a minimum of $10,000 to invest.

Certificates of Deposit (CDs)

CDs are bank, savings and loan, or credit union instruments that allow you to lock in an interest rate for a specific period of time. If you withdraw your money from the CD before the CD matures, you face an early-withdrawal penalty set by each bank – often three months' interest. The most popular CDs mature in three months, six months, and one year, although banks offer CDs with maturities as long as five years. Some banks even offer so-called "designer" CDs, for which you decide the maturity and the bank quotes you a yield. Generally, the longer you commit your money, the higher your CD's yield will be. Banks usually set some minimum amount for CDs, which can be as low as $100 or as much as $1,000, but they never charge a fee to buy a certificate.

There are several methods that banks use to pay interest on CDs. In many cases, the interest is not paid until the CD matures. For longer term CDs, banks mail out checks every three or six months, or they deposit the money directly into your bank account. Most banks will also allow you to reinvest your interest in the CD if you wish. All interest from CDs is taxable at the federal, state, and local levels in the year it is received, even if the interest is reinvested. Remember to calculate the effect of those taxes when you compare your potential CD returns against other alternatives, like tax-free money funds or municipal bonds.

Since the banking industry was deregulated in the 1980s, banks have been able to offer whatever rates they want on CDs. The yield that any particular bank is willing to pay depends on its executives' expectations of loan demand. If they expect a pickup in loan demand, they might raise the rates they pay on CDs to attract more funds to lend. If they do not see much demand for loans, they will not offer higher than market rates.

You do not have to restrict your search for high yields to your neighborhood or even your state. Many banks accept out-of-state deposits by wire or mail, and the highest yields around the country are publicized constantly in major financial newspapers such as *The Wall Street Journal* and *USA Today*, as well as the "Money Monitor" section of MONEY Magazine. You can also subscribe to the newsletter *100 Highest Yields* (P.O. Box 088888, North Palm Beach, FL 33408; 800-327-7717), which surveys banks every week to uncover those with the top yields for six-month, one-year, two-and-a-half year, and five-year certificates.

As with other bank products, different banks use different methods of compounding interest on their CDs. Some compound using simple interest, while others compound daily, weekly, monthly, quarterly, semiannually or annually. This affects what banks advertise as the "effective yield" on a CD, which, in fact, is mythical because it is unlikely that you would be able to capture exactly the same rate when the CD comes due in three or six months.

Make sure that you check with your bank to see what happens when your CD matures. Banks are not required to notify you when a CD is about to mature. Some will automatically reinvest the money in a new CD at the prevailing rate, which may or may not be what you want. Some banks will automatically mail you a check for the full amount of your CD, while others will put the money in a low-yielding passbook account until you give them further instructions.

To protect yourself against the ups and downs of interest rates, you might try a strategy called *laddering*. Instead of putting all your money in one CD with one maturity, spread it among several CDs maturing every few months. With this technique, CDs will constantly be maturing, which gives you the chance to reinvest at higher rates if rates have risen. If rates have fallen, you still have several CDs locked in at higher rates.

[TWO]

I n v e s t i n g   i n   S t o c k s

f you've never invested in stocks or have only limited experience with them, you might be harboring a common misperception of the stock market: It's a dangerous, volatile place where thousands of sophisticated professional traders and brokers lurk to steal your hard-earned money.

The reality of the stock market – if you learn a little about it – could not be further from that myth. There are millions of small investors like you who have been able to finance their dreams by successfully buying and holding for years shares of profitable companies and of mutual funds that buy such shares. Millions of other investors depend on the regular income they earn from their stock and mutual fund holdings.

Sure, stock prices go down at times, as well as up. Sometimes, as in the crash of October 19, 1987, they can plummet so fast that your heart palpitates. But this is the exception that proves the rule. If you look over the past few decades, prices of good-quality companies' stocks have invariably moved higher as shareholders are rewarded by the performance of the firms they own. As a device to increase your net worth so you can achieve your financial goals, stocks or stock mutual funds are your best investment over the long run (see Figure 3).

[How to Pick Winning Stocks]

Before you buy any stocks, remember that they are vehicles that can enable you to reach your financial goals. When you hear an exciting story about a hot growth stock, you may be tempted to put your life savings in it so you can become a quick millionaire. Resist the temptation. Most importantly, examine your tolerance for risk. Also remember to put stocks in their place in the investment pyramid (see Figure 1) so that you are diversified against loss, yet stand to gain.

Fig. ❸ 1925-1992 - Stocks, Bonds, Bills & Inflation

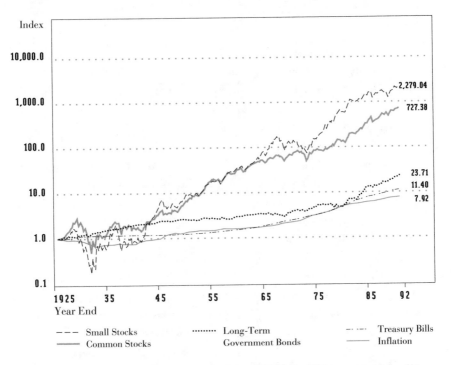

With that said, it's time to discuss the different techniques you can use to pick winning stocks. First, a few general tips that should help you make profitable decisions follow.

Plan to invest for the long term.
Despite endless predictions by market gurus that stocks are about to soar or plunge, no one really knows what will happen to stock prices over the short term. So, for the most part, you should ignore most of the prognostications. The same advice holds for the economy, which is just as unpredictable as the stock market.

Your emotions will probably get the best of you if you do a great deal of short-term trading. When prices are rising, you will tend to get caught up in the enthusiasm and buy more. When prices are falling, you will probably get depressed and sell out. Besides, excessive trading activity will generate hefty commissions for your broker and taxes on capital gains for Uncle Sam. Instead of trading for the short term, buy stocks that have good market positions, are financially strong, and offer products or services that seem sensible. If you can't explain what a company does in about two sentences, you probably shouldn't invest in it.

Buy stocks systematically.

Instead of putting all your money into a stock in one lump sum, buy a fixed dollar amount of shares on a regular basis, whether that be monthly, quarterly or annually. If you buy the same dollar amount of a stock, say $100 a month, you will automatically buy fewer shares when the price is high and more shares when the price is low, thereby assuring yourself of a low average price over time. This technique is known as *dollar cost averaging.* It's a lot safer and easier than trying to determine when a stock has hit its low or high point.

The following simple example demonstrates the value of dollar cost averaging (excluding the effect of commission costs).

If you have $10,000 to invest in a stock, either you could invest it all at once or, using dollar cost averaging, you could buy $1,000 worth every month for 10 months. The stock's price most surely will rise and fall over those 10 months, so let's say the stock starts the year at $50 a share, steadily descends to $25 a share by June 1, then returns to $50 a share by November 1. If you were to put your entire $10,000 to work in January, your results would look like Figure 4.

Fig. 4 Investing $10,000 All at the Same Time

Month	Amount Invested	Share Price	Shares Purchased	Cumulative Shares	Cumulative Market Value
January	$10,000	$50	200	200	$10,000
February	0	45	0	200	9,000
March	0	40	0	200	8,000
April	0	35	0	200	7,000
May	0	30	0	200	6,000
June	0	25	0	200	5,000
July	0	30	0	200	6,000
August	0	35	0	200	7,000
September	0	40	0	200	8,000
October	0	45	0	200	9,000
November	0	50	0	200	10,000
Total	$10,000	50*	200	200	$10,000

*average price

If, instead of investing all your money at once, you invested $1,000 on the first of every month, your results would look like Figure 5.

Fig. ⑤ Investing $10,000 by Dollar-Cost-Averaging Strategy

Month	Amount Invested	Share Price	Shares Purchased	Cumulative Shares	Cumulative Market Value
January	$1,000	$50	20	20	$1,000
February	1,000	45	22.2	42.2	1,899
March	1,000	40	25	67.2	2,688
April	1,000	35	28.5	95.7	3,349
May	1,000	30	33.3	129	3,870
June	1,000	25	40	169	4,225
July	1,000	30	33.3	202.3	6,069
August	1,000	35	28.5	230.8	8,078
September	1,000	40	25	255.8	10,232
October	1,000	45	22.2	278	12,510
November	0	50	0	278	13,900
Total	$10,000	$37.5*	278	278	$13,900

*average price

Notice that you would have ended up with $3,900 (or 39 percent) more if you had used the dollar-cost-averaging strategy than if you had bought all of your shares in January. The reason is that as the share price fell to a low of $25 on June 1, you kept buying more shares for your $1,000 each month. By the time the stock recovered back to the $50 level on November 1, you would have accumulated 78 more shares than if you had bought 200 shares in January. By buying 10 times instead of once, you would incur 10 commission charges, which would greatly reduce your gains. To avoid this problem, you can execute dollar-cost averaging using a no-load mutual fund (see Chapter 3 on mutual funds), or enroll in a company's dividend reinvestment plan (see later in this chapter), which allows you to buy shares commission-free and in fractional share amounts.

Figures 4 and 5 present a best-case scenario for dollar cost averaging because the price of the shares fell and then rebounded. Even in a less optimal case, where share prices rose and then dropped, you would still come out ahead with dollar cost averaging compared to investing all your money at once. That's the power of systematic investing!

Invest in stocks that you know well.

Use your professional knowledge to spot companies that seem to be up and coming. For example, if you are a doctor, what new drugs seem to be particularly effective, and who manufactured the new medical equipment that your hospital just installed? If you are a car mechanic, what company is making the best components for new cars? If you are a homemaker, what new stores seem to be crowded, and what new products seem to be hot sellers at the supermarket? You have many stock tips at your disposal. Use them for profit.

Research your choices carefully.

For some reason, people will spend weeks investigating every feature of a car costing $15,000, but when it comes to stocks, they will spend $15,000 based on a hot tip, a broker's recommendation or a mention in a newspaper story. Before you invest any money, know exactly what business the company is in, how profitable it is, whether it has much debt, which companies are competing with it, and what new products or services the company intends to introduce. Most of all, look at who is running the company. Firms can have great plans, but they need top-quality management to transform those plans into profitable reality. The best way to judge management is by looking at its track record. If the management team has succeeded in the past, chances are that the team can do it again.

Monitor the company after you've bought shares.

Read the quarterly and annual reports to see whether your projections are, in fact, coming to pass. Was the new product line successful? Did the company pay down its debt as you thought it would? Also keep an eye on the company's stock price. You don't need to check it every day – maybe once a week or at least once a month. If the stock price rises or falls dramatically, someone knows something about the stock that you will probably find out later. Also, you shouldn't own so many stocks that you don't have time to track them all. It's possible to be overdiversified as well as underdiversified.

Don't be pressured to buy or sell just because everyone else is doing so.

In fact, if everyone else is doing it, it's probably the wrong time to be joining in. It takes courage, but you will most likely make the bulk of your money by buying stocks when they are down and everyone dislikes them and by selling them when they are rising and every taxi cab driver lets you in on this latest "hot" tip.

Don't worry about missing out on a good stock.

The best ones rise in value for years at a time, so you have plenty of opportunity to get in on them. If you had bought Wal-Mart stock any time in the early 1970s, you would have made more than 30 times your money by the early 1990s. Just because a good stock moves up a few dollars, it's not too late to invest.

Have a selling target price in mind when you buy a stock.

If the stock reaches that price, either you can sell some or all of it, or you can reconsider your position based on the company's situation at that time. You should also know the price at which you would sell the stock at a loss. This might be between 25 percent and 50 percent less than you paid for it. One of the worst things you can do is to watch your stock's price melt away as you hope it will recover. Remember, your stock does not know or care what price you paid for it, so it has no obligation to return to that price.

Consider transaction costs before you buy.
If you have only enough money to buy a few shares, the commission you will pay might not be worth the investment. Determine in advance whether you will buy the stock through a full-service broker, who offers advice but charges higher fees, or a discount broker, who only executes your order but at much lower commission rates.

[Categories of Stock]

There are many kinds of stocks, and some are more appropriate for you than others, depending on your risk profile and financial objectives. We will concentrate here on five categories of stocks (cyclical, growth, income, out-of-favor, and value) and provide worksheets that will tell you whether a stock you are interested in passes the test.

Cyclical Stocks

Certain companies' fortunes are very closely tied to the ups and downs of the economy, and if you time purchases and sales of such company stocks well, you can profit handsomely. Cyclical stocks, so called because they ride the economic cycle, are typically found in such heavy industries as auto manufacturing, paper, chemicals, steel, and aluminum. These companies all have relatively large fixed costs to run their factories. As a result, if the volume of the product they sell is high and the prices they receive are rising because of strong demand, they stand to cover those costs easily and earn enormous profits. However, when demand is weak and prices are falling, they are still burdened by the same costs, so their earnings plummet.

Cyclical stock prices are even more volatile than the company's earnings. Investors are constantly trying to determine whether the cycle is turning up or down because it has a tremendous impact on the company's bottom line. While all stock prices reflect investors' expectations of future profits, cyclical stocks are even more sensitive to perceptions about the future.

The best time to buy cyclical stocks, as hard as it may be to do, is when they are still losing money in the bottom of a recession but their situation is no longer deteriorating. The moment that investors sense a turnaround, the stock

Fig. **6** Cyclical Stock Worksheet

	Sample Stock Points	Your Stock Points

Sample Stock

$$\frac{\text{Current stock price} \quad = \$40}{\text{Stock price at last cyclical peak} \quad = \$60} = 66\%$$

Your Stock

$$\frac{\text{Current stock price} \quad = \$}{\text{Stock price at last cyclical peak} \quad = \$} = \quad \%$$

(If less than 75%, give your stock 2 points; if between 75% and 100%, 1 point; if more than 100%, 0 points.)   **2** _____

Sample Stock

$$\frac{\text{PE ratio at last cyclical peak} \quad = \quad 20}{\text{PE ratio now} \quad = \quad 25} = 80\%$$

Your Stock

$$\frac{\text{PE ratio at last cyclical peak} \quad =}{\text{PE ratio now} \quad =} = \quad \%$$

(If less than 50%, give your stock 2 points; if between 50% and 80%, 1 point; if more than 80%, 0 points.)   **1** _____

Sample Stock

$$\frac{\text{Estimated sales gain for next quarter} \quad = 20\%}{\text{Gain for same quarter a year ago} \quad = 10\%} = 200\%$$

Your Stock

$$\frac{\text{Estimated sales gain for next quarter} \quad = \quad \%}{\text{Gain for same quarter a year ago} \quad = \quad \%} = \quad \%$$

(If more than 125%, give your stock 2 points; if between 100% and 125%, 1 point; if less than 100%, 0 points.)   **2** _____

Source: Reprinted from MONEY Guide/The Stock Market – 1986, by special permission; © 1986, Time, Inc.

Fig. 6 continued

	Sample Stock Points	Your Stock Points

Sample Stock

$$\frac{\text{Next year's estimated profit margin} = 10\%}{\text{This year's estimated profit margin} = 7\%} = 143\%$$

Your Stock

$$\frac{\text{Next year's estimated profit margin} = \quad\%}{\text{This year's estimated profit margin} = \quad\%} = \quad\%$$

(If more than 125%, give your stock 2 points; if between
100% and 125%, 1 point; if less than 100%, 0 points.)   2   _____

Sample Stock

$$\frac{\text{Next year's estimated return on equity} = 15\%}{\text{This year's return on equity} = 10\%} = 150\%$$

Your Stock

$$\frac{\text{Next year's estimated return on equity} = \quad\%}{\text{This year's return on equity} = \quad\%} = \quad\%$$

(If more than 125%, give your stock 2 points; if between
100% and 125%, 1 point; if less than 100%, 0 points.)   2   _____

Total Points   9   _____

If your stock scores 6 points or more, you have probably found a cyclical stock
about to take off. The example here is clearly a good investment.

---

will shoot up. Conversely, the time to sell a cyclical stock is when the company
is earning record profits and everything seems to be going well. When
investors sense that the rate of improvement is slowing or growth is stalling,
the stock will decline rapidly.

The worksheet in Figure 6 will help you evaluate where a cyclical stock is
in its cycle and, therefore, whether now is a good time to buy it. All the numbers needed to complete this worksheet (and those on the following pages)
are available from Standard & Poor's company profiles or the *Value Line
Investment Survey*. We have provided sample numbers for a cyclical stock.

Growth Stocks

The easiest way for most people to make money in stocks over the long term is to buy and hold shares in high-quality growth companies. If it is a true growth stock, its earnings will compound at 15 percent or more no matter what the overall economy is doing. Impossible, you say? Take a look at the track records of such stellar growth companies as tax preparation giant H&R Block, retailer Wal-Mart, tobacco and food company Philip Morris, and software king Microsoft, for starters.

Growth stocks can perform so admirably because their companies offer proprietary niche products or services and have well-known brand names, strong finances, and top-flight management. As long as these factors remain constant, growth can continue indefinitely. At a certain point, though, as a company becomes huge, it is more difficult to generate the same percentage profit increases; however, some firms seem to keep the increases coming, despite the odds.

Fig. 7 Growth Stock Worksheet

	Sample Stock Points	Your Stock Points
Sample Stock		
Projected five-year annual growth rate =	22%	
Your Stock		
Projected five-year annual growth rate =	%	
(If more than 20%, give your stock 2 points; if between 10% and 20%, 1 point; if less than 10%, 0 points.)	2	
Sample Stock		
Earnings growth rate for last five years =	25%	
Your Stock		
Earnings growth rate for last five years =	%	
(If more than 20%, give your stock 2 points; if between 10% and 20%, 1 point; if less than 10%, 0 points.)	2	

Source: Reprinted from MONEY Guide/The Stock Market – 1986, by special permission; © 1986, Time, Inc.

Fig. 7 continued

	Sample Stock Points	Your Stock Points

Sample Stock

Average return on equity for past three years   =   18%

Your Stock

Average return on equity for past three years   =   %

(If more than 20%, give your stock 2 points; if between
10% and 20%, 1 point; if less than 10%, 0 points.)   1   _____

Sample Stock

$$\frac{\text{Projected five-year earnings growth rate} = 22\%}{\text{Stock's current PE ratio} \qquad = 16\%} = 137\%$$

Your Stock

$$\frac{\text{Projected five-year earnings growth rate} = \quad\%}{\text{Stock's current PE ratio} \qquad = \quad\%} = \quad\%$$

(If more than 160%, give your stock 2 points; if between
125% and 160%, 1 point; if less than 125%, 0 points.)   1   _____

Sample Stock

Earnings consistency = Up   7% in each of last five years

Your Stock

Earnings consistency = Up   % in each of last five years
(If up 10% or more for each of the last five years, give your stock
2 points; if up for each of the last five years, give your stock
1 point; if down in any of the last five years, 0 points.)   1   _____

Total Points   7

If your stock scores 6 points or more, it has long-term growth potential. The
example here looks like an attractive growth stock.

So far, investing in growth stocks sounds like a breeze. But it isn't quite that easy. The better the record a growth company establishes, the higher investors' expectations soar, and the higher the stock's price-earnings (PE) ratio climbs. As long as the growth continues unabated, no problem occurs. But the moment such a company reports a slight slip in its upward trajectory, the stock can take a seemingly senseless pounding. As we stated earlier, one of the last investments you want to own is growth stock about to disappoint investors' earnings expectations. Also, successful companies attract imitators, which usually try to copy the original company's products or services and sell them cheaper. Sometimes that can slow the company's profit growth.

One of the biggest mistakes people make when buying growth stocks is to get too excited by their prospects and pay too much for the stocks. An easy way to judge whether you are overpaying is to look at the stock's PE ratio. The higher the PE ratio, the more enthusiastic investors are about the company. Compare the PE ratio of your stock with that of similar companies in the same industry. If your stock's PE ratio is considerably higher, you could be paying too much.

The other key indicator growth stock investors look for is the *earnings growth rate*, or the rate at which profits grow from year to year. In general, the higher the growth rate, the higher the stock's PE ratio. The ideal growth stock is one selling at a PE ratio below its growth rate. For example, if Go-Go Computer's profits are growing at 30 percent a year, its stock would be considered a bargain if it were selling for a PE ratio of 20. While producing a solid growth rate is important, consistent growth is also highly prized. A company with profits up 40 percent one year and down 20 percent the next will not earn as high a PE ratio as one that grows 20 percent year after year.

The worksheet in Figure 7 will help you evaluate your own growth stock. All the numbers needed to complete this worksheet are available from Standard & Poor's company profiles or the *Value Line Investment Survey*. We have provided sample numbers for a growth stock.

Income Stocks

While most people think of stocks as vehicles to achieve capital appreciation, they can also provide steady income. Good-quality income stocks have an advantage over bonds for income investors. While the interest that a bond pays is fixed until the bond matures, a stock's dividend can rise year after year. So although a bond usually provides a higher current yield, a stock with a solid record of dividend increases can actually pay more over time. Because those higher dividends are paid out of ever-increasing profits, the stock price should climb over time as well.

Companies that pay high dividends usually are well-established, profitable firms. Some businesses that offer high-paying stocks include banking firms, real estate investment trusts, and electric, gas, telephone, and water utilities. Unlike faster-growing younger companies, which reinvest profits in their own businesses, such firms traditionally pay out at least half their profits to shareholders in the form of dividends.

Fig. (8) Income Stock Worksheet

		Sample Stock Points	Your Stock Points
Sample Stock			
Dividend yield	= 7%		
Your Stock			
Dividend yield	= %		
(If more than 6%, give your stock 2 points; if between 4% and 6%, 1 point; if less than 4%, 0 points.)		2	_____
Sample Stock			
Dividend growth rate for last five years	= 9%		
Your Stock			
Dividend growth rate for last five years	= %		
(If more than 8%, give your stock 2 points; if between 5% and 8%, 1 point; if less than 5%, 0 points.)		2	_____
Sample Stock			
Projected five-year earnings growth rate	= 10%		
Your Stock			
Projected five-year earnings growth rate	= %		
(If more than 8%, give your stock 2 points; if between 5% and 8%, 1 point; if less than 5%, 0 points.)		2	_____

Source: Reprinted from MONEY Guide/The Stock Market – 1986, by special permission; © 1986, Time, Inc.

Fig. 8 continued

	Sample Stock Points	Your Stock Points

Sample Stock

$$\frac{\text{Dividends per common share} = \quad \$1}{\text{Earnings per common share} \;=\; \$2} = \begin{array}{l} 50\% \text{ Dividend} \\ \text{payout ratio} \end{array}$$

Your Stock

$$\frac{\text{Dividends per common share} = \quad \$}{\text{Earnings per common share} \;=} = \begin{array}{l} \% \text{ Dividend} \\ \text{payout ratio} \end{array}$$

(If less than 60%, give your stock 2 points; if between 60% and 70%, 1 point; if more than 70%, 0 points.)   2   _____

Sample Stock

Financial strength rating   = A-

Your Stock

Financial strength rating   =
(If the credit agency's rating is A or above, give
your stock 2 points, if between B+ and A-,
1 point; if lower than B+, 0 points.)   1   _____

Total Points   9   _____

If your stock scores 6 points or more, it should provide steady attractive income. The example here is a stock that any retiree could count on to pay uninterrupted dividends for years.

Even more than prices of other stocks, high-yield stock prices are greatly influenced by the direction of interest rates. When rates on Treasury bonds fall, high-yield stock prices tend to rise because that stock's dividends are more competitive with bonds. Conversely, when interest rates rise, high-yield stocks look less attractive, and their prices tend to drop.

To make sure an income stock you are considering can continue to raise its dividend, you should determine that the company is financially strong. You can do this by analyzing the company's debt. Debt that is more than 50 percent of the company's equity may be a sign of trouble. Another quick way to gauge financial strength is to check the stock's rating with a reputable credit rating agency's ratings, such as *Standard & Poor's Stock Guide.* Any rating over B+ means that the company is financially solid.

The final ratio to inspect before you buy a stock for income is the *payout ratio*, the percentage of earnings that is paid out in dividends. A payout ratio below 60 percent means that there is a sizable cushion for the company to fall back on before it has to cut its dividend. A low ratio also leaves room for the dividend to grow. On the other hand, a payout ratio above 60 percent might be a sign that the dividend may be cut.

Don't be entranced by a stock that sports an above-average yield, usually of more than 10 percent. There must be a reason why the yield is that high, and probably it is not positive. For example, the payout may be high because the stock price has fallen in anticipation of a dividend cut. Or it may be high because the company is in the process of liquidation, and the high payouts are actually a return of shareholders' capital. Whatever the reason, be suspicious of stocks with ultra-high yields.

Out-of-Favor Stocks

If the age-old way to make money in stocks is to buy low and sell high, then buying stocks when they are out of favor is a good way to buy low. Though this style of choosing stocks can be emotionally trying, it can be rewarding as well. Investors are not always rational. Just as they can bid up the price of a growth stock too high because they are so enthusiastic about its prospects, they can also pummel a stock that has momentarily slipped to unrealistically low prices. That's where bargain hunters swoop in. They sell out when the stock recovers.

The easiest way to spot neglected stocks is by looking for low PE ratios. A PE ratio of less than 10 signals that investors do not have much hope for the future of the company, which may, in fact, be an incorrect perception of the situation. The moment the company reports better-than-expected results, perceptions can change quickly, and the stock price can shoot up. Do your research first. Don't be tempted to buy just any stock with a low PE ratio, however. Some companies deserve their lowly valuation and, in fact, will not recover.

In addition to a low PE ratio, bargain hunters usually look for industries that are currently out of favor. They also seek stocks with low price-book value ratios because such stocks are typically out of favor. Another sign of benign neglect is when few of the shares are held by institutional investors, such as mutual funds or banks, because it is not fashionable to own such depressed stocks. Finally, if brokerage analysts do not pay attention to a stock, it is probably out of favor.

What you *should* look for is a stock with a fair chance at turnaround. You may infer that a recovery is on the way if sales and earnings are no longer deteriorating or if the company has a new product or service that has the potential to restart its growth. Another way to check for signs of life is to determine whether company executives are buying the stock themselves and whether they are increasing capital expenditures. If the people who know the company best are investing in it heavily, that could be a tip-off that recovery is at hand.

Not every ugly duckling turns into a swan, however. If your stock remains depressed after a year or more, you probably should turn it in for another one. It takes only one or two dramatic recoveries for this strategy to pay off.

Fig. ❾ Out-of-Favor Stock Worksheet

	Sample Stock Points	Your Stock Points

Sample Stock

$$\frac{\text{Current stock price} = \$40}{\text{Book value per share} = \$90} = 44\%$$

Your Stock

$$\frac{\text{Current stock price} = \$}{\text{Book value per share} = \$} = \quad\%$$

(If less than 25%, give your stock 2 points; if between 25% and 50%, 1 point; if more than 50%, 0 points.)   1   _____

Sample Stock

$$\frac{\text{Stock PE ratio} = 10}{\text{S \& P 500 PE ratio} = 15} = 66\%$$

Your Stock

$$\frac{\text{Stock PE ratio} =}{\text{S \& P 500 PE ratio} =} = \quad\%$$

(If less than 80%, give your stock 2 points; if between 80% and 100%, 1 point; if more than 100%, 0 points.)   2   _____

Source: Reprinted from MONEY Guide/The Stock Market – 1986, by special permission; © 1986, Time, Inc.

Fig. 9 continued

	Sample Stock Points	*Your Stock Points*

Sample Stock

Estimated five-year earnings growth rate   =   6%

Your Stock

Estimated five-year earnings growth rate   =   %

(If more than 7%, give your stock 2 points; if between
2% and 7%, 1 point; if less than 2%, 0 points.)   1

Sample Stock

$$\frac{\text{Estimated capital expenditures for this year} = \$50 \text{ million}}{\text{Capital expenditures for last year} = \$20 \text{ million}} = 250\%$$

Your Stock

$$\frac{\text{Estimated capital expenditures for this year} = \$ \quad \text{million}}{\text{Capital expenditures for last year} = \$ \quad \text{million}} = \quad \%$$

(If more than 150%, give your stock 2 points; if between
100% and 150%, 1 point; if less than 100%, 0 points.)   2

Sample Stock

Percentage of outstanding stock held by institutions =   30%

Your Stock

Percentage of outstanding stock held by institutions =   %

(If less than 25%, give your stock 2 points; if between
25% and 50%, 1 point; if more than 50%, 0 points.)   1

Total Points   7

If your stock scores 6 points or more, you might have uncovered a worthy out-of-favor stock. The example here is a stock that has been neglected, yet shows signs of a rebound. That means that its stock price should recover soon.

All the numbers needed to complete the worksheet in Figure 9 are available from Standard & Poor's company profiles or the *Value Line Investment Survey*. We have provided sample numbers for an out-of-favor stock.

Value Stocks

If you could buy a stock worth $10 for $8, would you do it? Most people would because they know they are buying something for less than it is worth. In the stock market, this style of choosing stocks is known as *value investing*.

The key to value investing is being able to perceive when a stock's current price does not fully reflect the value of its assets. Those assets might include real estate, brand names, oil reserves, patented technology, or even cash or stocks in other companies. Value investors make money by buying when the stock's assets are worth more than the stock's price and selling when the value of the assets has been realized.

Shareholders can be paid for the true value of their company's assets in one of several ways. A company can be taken over by another company or by a raider at a premium price because the acquirer thinks it can sell the assets for even more. The company can be broken into pieces, leaving shareholders with several stocks worth more separately than they were worth as a whole. The company's management can derive a way to make the formerly underused asset more productive, which would produce profits to boost the stock price. Or investors can finally realize the value of the company's assets, and the stock price will rise to reflect that changed perception.

Trying to determine the true value of assets is tricky and subjective. A valuable asset to one analyst may have far less worth to another. Still, you can get a sense of whether a stock is selling for less than its breakup value by looking at the company's book value per share, tangible assets per share like land or oil reserves, and financial assets, including cash and securities. A particularly stringent test is to compare the stock's price to so-called *net net working capital.* That is the amount of cash a company could raise in a hurry if it were liquidated today. To calculate it, subtract short- and long-term debts from such current assets as cash, securities, receivables, and inventory. If the net net working capital of the stock you are looking at is 25 percent or more than the current price, you have found an undervalued stock.

The other way to identify a value stock is to see how much it would be worth if it continued in business. Take a look at the firm's cash flow (profits plus depreciation) per share, and divide it by the current stock price. The lower the price-cash flow ratio, the cheaper the stock is. At a certain point, the cash the company is throwing off could finance an acquisition of the company, making it a likely takeover target.

Fig. ⑩ Value Stock Worksheet

	Sample Stock Points	Your Stock Points

Sample Stock

$$\frac{\text{Current stock price} \quad = \$40}{\text{Book value per share} \quad = \$45} = 89\%$$

Your Stock

$$\frac{\text{Current stock price} \quad = \$}{\text{Book value per share} \quad = \$} = \quad\%$$

(If less than 100%, give your stock 2 points; if between 100% and 140%, 1 point; if more than 140%, 0 points.)

2 _____   _____

Sample Stock

$$\frac{\text{Cash per share} \quad = \$\ 5}{\text{Current stock price} \quad = \$40} = 12.5\%$$

Your Stock

$$\frac{\text{Cash per share} \quad = \$}{\text{Current stock price} \quad = \$} = \quad\%$$

(If more than 25%, give your stock 2 points; if between 10% and 25%, 1 point; if less than 10%, 0 points.)

1 _____   _____

Sample Stock

$$\frac{\text{Net net working capital per share} \quad = \$\ 6}{\text{Current stock price} \quad = \$40} = 15\%$$

Your Stock

$$\frac{\text{Net net working capital per share} \quad = \$}{\text{Current stock price} \quad = \$} = \quad\%$$

(If more than 25%, give your stock 2 points; if between 0% and 25%, 1 point; if less than 0%, 0 points.)

1 _____   _____

Source: Reprinted from MONEY Guide/The Stock Market – 1986, by special permission; © 1986, Time, Inc.

Fig. 10 continued

	Sample Stock Points	Your Stock Points

Sample Stock

$$\frac{\text{Current stock price} \quad = \$40}{\text{Cash flow per share} \quad = \$10} = 4$$

Your Stock

$$\frac{\text{Current stock price} \quad = \$}{\text{Cash flow per share} \quad = \$} =$$

(If less than 5, give your stock 2 points; if between 5 and 7, 1 point; if more than 7, 0 points.)

| | 2 | ___ |

Sample Stock

$$\frac{\text{Outstanding debt} \quad = \$\ 19 \text{ million}}{\text{Total capital} \quad = \$100 \text{ million}} = 19\%$$

Your Stock

$$\frac{\text{Outstanding debt} \quad = \$\quad \text{million}}{\text{Total capital} \quad = \$\quad \text{million}} = \quad\%$$

(If less than 20%, give your stock 2 points; if between 20% and 30%, 1 point; if more than 30%, 0 points.)

| | 2 | ___ |

Total Points

| | 8 | ___ |

If your stock scores 4 points or more, you might be looking at an undervalued stock. The example here is a real bargain.

All the numbers needed to fill out the worksheet in Figure 10 are available from Standard & Poor's company profiles or the *Value Line Investment Survey.*

[Dividend Reinvestment Plans (DRIPs)]

If you own a stock that is paying a dividend, chances are that the company offers a terrific benefit called a *dividend reinvestment plan,* commonly known as a DRIP. If you don't need the cash from your dividend to live on, you can reinvest the payment with the company and buy more shares of stock. About 1,000 companies offer a DRIP.

Enrolling in a DRIP offers several advantages.

You put the magic of compounding to work for you. The shares that you buy with reinvested dividends earn more dividends, which buy more shares, and so on. Over time, the number of shares you own in the company grows steadily, without your having to contribute more cash.

Without even thinking about it, you are practicing dollar cost averaging. For example, say you receive $100 in dividends each quarter. When the share price is high, like $50, your dividends will buy fewer shares – in this case, two shares. But when the share price is low, like $20, the same dividends will buy more shares – in this case, five. This counteracts your normal emotional inclination to buy more shares when the price is high and rising and fewer when the price is low and falling. Over time, your average cost of buying shares will most likely be lower than it would be if you tried to time your purchases.

Most DRIPs are free of brokerage commissions and other charges. Because the company offering the plan wants to encourage shareholders to use it, the firm normally absorbs all brokerage commissions for buying the stock and the administrative costs of the program.

About 100 companies offer a sweetened version of the DRIP, called a discount DRIP. To encourage shareholder participation, the company gives up to an additional 5 percent discount on reinvested dividends. So, for example, if you reinvest $100 worth of dividends, you receive $105 worth of stock. This makes your holdings in the company grow even faster.

The following is a sample of the companies that offer a 5 percent discount on reinvested dividends, provided courtesy of Charles Carlson, author of *Buying Stocks Without a Broker* and *Free Lunch on Wall Street: Perks, Freebies, and Giveaways for Investors* (both by McGraw-Hill, Order Dept., Monterey Ave., Blue Ridge Summit, PA 17294; 800-233-1128). The books explain how DRIPs work and provide a directory of all plans, including a profile of each company, with its address and telephone number, whether it offers optional cash purchase plans, and other details of its plans. Carlson is also editor of the monthly newsletter *The DRIP Investor* (Dow Theory Forecasts, 7412 Calumet Ave., Hammond, IN 46324; 219-931-6480). The newsletter keeps an updated list of such plans.

Several hundred companies not only allow you to reinvest your dividends; they offer optional cash purchase plans. These plans enable you to invest your own money, along with your dividends, in more shares at no cost. While that alone is a great deal, some firms even offer optional cash purchase at a discount. The companies that offer a 5 percent DRIP discount also extend the discount to any additional money you invest. Most of these programs, however, put limits on optional cash purchases, usually of about $25,000 a year. (The companies don't want to give away too much free money, after all.)

American Water Works Company
Aquarion Company
Ball Corporation
Baltimore Bancorp
Bancorp Hawaii, Inc.
Bankers First Corporation
BB&T Financial Corporation
Blount, Inc.
BMJ Financial Corporation
Boulevard Bancorp, Inc.
Burnham Pacific Properties, Inc.
California Real Estate Investment Trust
Central Maine Power Company
Chase Manhattan Corporation
Colonial Gas Company
Connecticut Water Service, Inc.
Crestar Financial Corporation
Eastern Utilities Associates
Empire District Electric Company
EnergyNorth, Inc.
E'Town Corporation
F & M National Corporation
First American Corporation
First Commerce Corporation
First Eastern Corporation
First Michigan Bank Corporation
First of America Bank Corporation
Fleet Financial Group, Inc.
Fleming Companies, Inc.
Huntington Bancshares, Inc.
Inco Ltd.
Independence Bancorp
Independent Bank Corporation

IRT Property Company
Jefferson Bankshares, Inc.
Kennametal, Inc.
Lafarge Corporation
Mercantile Bankshares Corporation
Meridian Bancorp, Inc.
Merry Land & Investment Company, Inc.
NationsBank Corporation
New Plan Realty Trust
North Carolina Natural Gas Corp.
North Fork Bancorporation, Inc.
NUI Corporation
Philadelphia Suburban Corporation
Piccadilly Cafeterias, Inc.
Piedmont Natural Gas Company, Inc.
Presidential Realty Corporation
Public Service Company of North Carolina
Signet Banking Corporation
Southwestern Electric Service Company
Southwest Water Company
Telephone & Data Systems, Inc.
Texas Utilities Company
Time Warner, Inc.
Timken Company
TransCanada Pipelines Ltd.
UGI Corporation
Union Bank
Union Planters Corporation
United Cities Gas Company
United Water Resources, Inc.
Utilicorp United, Inc.
Washington National Corporation
Westcoast Energy, Inc.

Several companies not only allow you to reinvest dividends and optional cash at no charge; they also make it easy to buy your original shares directly from the companies themselves, without commissions. Theoretically, you could buy shares in these firms, enroll in their DRIPs and optional cash programs, and build up a stake of hundreds of shares without ever paying a commission! (Don't tell your broker that you know about this one, or he or she won't return your calls!)

Following is a partial list of the companies allowing direct initial stock purchases. This list, too, is provided by Charles Carlson, editor of *The DRIP Investor* newsletter, which maintains a current list of such plans. Carlson refers to stocks obtained through these plans as no-load stocks.™

American Recreation Centers, Inc.; 916-852-8005
Arrow Financial Corporation; 518-793-4121
Atlantic Energy; 609-645-4506
Atmos Energy Corporation; 800-382-8667
Central Vermont Public Service Corporation;
802-773-2711
Citizens First Bancorp, Inc.; 201-670-2456
DQE; 800-247-0400

Exxon Corporation; 800-252-1800
First Alabama Bancshares, Inc.; 800-638-6431
W. R. Grace & Company; 800-851-9677
Interchange Financial Services; 201-703-2265
Johnson Controls, Inc.; 414-287-3956
SCANA Corporation; 800-763-5891
Texaco, Inc.; 800-283-9785

To enroll in a company's dividend reinvestment plan, you must have the stock registered in your own name. Normally, if you buy stock through a brokerage firm, the broker holds it in its *street name* – that is, under a consolidated name for all of its accounts. A company offering a DRIP, however, must know the name of the participating shareholder so it can set up a reinvestment account. Therefore, if you have your stock with a broker, you must reregister it with the company, which the company will gladly take care of for you. After you're enrolled in the plan, you will receive quarterly statements from the company informing you how many shares your dividends purchased and how many total shares you now own.

[S h a r e h o l d e r   F r e e b i e s]

In addition to dividends and DRIPs, many companies offer shareholders a variety of free and discounted products and services, which can make buying a company's stock even more rewarding. Companies do this to engender good will among their shareholders and to encourage them to hold onto their stock for the long term.

In some cases, you must attend the annual meeting, where the freebies are handed out to – or, in some cases, devoured by – shareholders. In other cases, you can receive discount coupons or tickets by writing to the company. To learn what a specific company offers, call its investor relations department. To learn about benefits in general, consult the latest edition of Gene Walden's book, *The 100 Best Stocks To Own in America* (Dearborn Financial Publishing, 520 N. Dearborn St., Chicago, IL 60610; 800-322-8621). With his permission, the following are a few benefits companies now offer:

Abbott Laboratories. At the annual meeting, shareholders receive a sampling of Abbott's consumer products, such as Selsun Blue, Murine, an ice pack, and a bottle of vitamins.

Albertson's, Inc. At the annual meeting, shareholders receive some of Albertson's private label groceries, including canned vegetables, napkins, paper towels, and other household products.

American Home Products Corp. Occasionally, the company sends out coupons for some of its foods and health care products along with the dividend check.

Anheuser-Busch Companies, Inc. New shareholders of record are sent a letter of welcome, a fact book on the company, and a pamphlet on its dividend reinvestment plan. The company makes a point of moving its annual meetings around the country. Those who attend get a chance to sample all the company's brews. Shareholders are also entitled to a discount on admission to the company's amusement parks.

Bristol-Myers Squibb. The company sends all new shareholders a welcome packet of its consumer products, including, for example, small bottles of Excedrin, Bufferin, Nuprin, Clairol hair care products, and Ban deodorant.

Campbell Soup Company. The company hands out a bag of freebies at the annual meeting, including coupons, soup, cookies, chicken nuggets, Vlasic pickles, and some new product samples.

Circus Circus Enterprises, Inc. At the annual meeting, the company traditionally passes out small gifts to shareholders, such as a special coin set or free tokens for the slot machines.

ConAgra, Inc. At the annual meeting, the company passes out a gift pack of some of its foods to shareholders, and it sometimes sends out discount offers along with its quarterly earnings reports.

Corning, Inc. Corning sends discount cards to all of its shareholders each year offering a 30 percent discount on Corning merchandise (including Steubenware crystal) purchased at the company's corporate headquarters, and 10 percent off merchandise purchased at stores. At the annual meeting, the company serves lunch and hands out a product sample.

Deluxe Corp. Deluxe offers no dividend reinvestment plan, but it does offer one perk. At the annual meeting, shareholders are invited to a dinner – on the company – after the meeting. Meetings rotate around six locations: St. Paul, Chicago, Kansas City, Houston, Los Angeles, and New Jersey, where the company has a large concentration of shareholders.

The Walt Disney Company. For a limited time, shareholders qualify for a 20 percent discount on the Magic Kingdom Club Gold Card. Gold Card membership provides a wide range of benefits, including savings on admission at the theme parks and select resort hotel accommodations, and discounts on travel arrangements with Delta Air, National Car Rental, and Premier Cruise Lines. Gold Card members also receive a personalized, embossed membership card, an informative newsletter, a two-year subscription to *Disney News* magazine, a Disney vacation planning video, and a toll-free number for the Magic Kingdom Club Travel Centers.

General Mills, Inc. General Mills occasionally sends out coupons for some of its products along with its quarterly reports. It also offers holiday gift boxes in

December at very attractive prices. In 1992, for example, the boxes included nearly $50 worth of goods and coupons.

H. J. Heinz Company. At the annual meeting, shareholders receive a gift package of some of the company's newer products. The company puts out one of corporate America's best quarterly reports. Generally about 30 pages, the reports are packed with new product information and company developments. They also occasionally carry special offers or product discounts for Heinz shareholders.

Hershey Foods Corp. The company makes Christmas shopping a lot easier for shareholders with chocolate-loving friends. Hershey's Chocolate World Visitors Center mails its Christmas gift catalog to any shareholder requesting it and maintains a mailing list for annual receipt of the catalog. Shareholders may purchase special gift packages from the catalog and have them wrapped and mailed directly to their friends. At the annual meeting, shareholders are treated to a free packet of Hershey's candies and pasta.

International Dairy Queen, Inc. At the annual meeting, the company serves some of its Brazier foods and newer ice cream products.

Kellogg Company. All new shareholders of record receive a welcome kit with brochures and reports on the company along with a pair of coupons for free grocery products. At the annual meeting in Battle Creek, shareholders also receive product samples and discount coupons. The company sometimes hands out special gifts, such as decorative Kellogg's plates.

The Limited, Inc. The company sent out a coupon with its most recent annual report for 15 percent off merchandise at any of its stores.

Loctite Corp. At the annual meeting, the company hands out tubes of Super Glue.

McDonald's Corp. A wealth of literature on McDonald's and its locations and product ingredients is available to shareholders (or anyone else requesting it). The company also provides an investor hot-line (not toll-free) that gives company news.

Newell Corp. At the annual meeting, the company often hands out a special gift. At a recent meeting, shareholders received a glass vase from the Anchor Hocking glassware division.

Nike, Inc. Each year at the annual meeting, the company passes out some promotional items. Don't expect to walk away in a pair of Air Jordans, but at a recent meeting, shareholders took home a cap like the one worn by tennis star Andre Agassi, a sports towel, and a Nike pen.

Quaker Oats Company. Coupons for a percentage off some of Quaker's new products are often sent to shareholders along with their quarterly reports. The company puts out one of corporate America's best quarterly and annual reports. At the annual meeting, shareholders are sometimes given sample packets of some of Quaker's newer products.

Rubbermaid Inc. At the annual meeting, shareholders usually receive a free Rubbermaid product, such as a file case, food tray, or food storage container. Shareholders may also shop in the company store on annual meeting day and may take advantage of discounts on dozens of Rubbermaid products.

Sara Lee Corp. Each year at the annual meeting, Sara Lee shareholders receive a gift box of Sara Lee products, including such items as coupons, bath soaps and other company products.

Schering-Plough Corp. Schering-Plough gives a sample packet of products to shareholders at its annual meetings. The packets include such products as Coppertone sun tan lotion, Afrin nasal spray, Gyne-Lotrimin, and other over-the-counter remedies.

Stanhome, Inc. At the annual meeting, the company hands out a gift pack of product samples, such as a collectible item, Stanley cologne, and other personal care products.

UST, Inc. At the annual meeting, the company hands out samples of its products, such as pipe cleaners, a pipe, smokeless tobacco, a small bottle of wine, and a video from its new Cabin Fever Entertainment subsidiary.

Walgreen Company. At the annual meeting, shareholders usually receive one or two Walgreen products.

Wal-Mart Stores, Inc. At the annual meeting, shareholders are often given Wal-Mart memorabilia, such as hats, buttons, and T-shirts.

William Wrigley Jr. Company. Wrigley sends out to shareholders a gift package each Christmas that includes several packs of Wrigley's gum.

[THREE]

Selecting the Best Mutual Funds

[Stock Mutual Funds]

I f the process of selecting individual stocks seems a bit overwhelming, one alternative offers the benefits of stock ownership without the complications of choosing stocks: mutual funds that invest in stocks.

Mutual funds, which have been around since the 1920s, have, in recent years, blossomed into the most commonly used vehicle for average Americans to own stocks. That's because they are easy to use and understand, and they provide several great services at a low cost.

Put simply, a stock mutual fund is a pool of money that a fund manager invests in stocks to achieve a specific objective. The fund is sponsored by a mutual fund company, which may be an independent firm, such as Fidelity, T. Rowe Price, or Vanguard, or a division of a brokerage or insurance company, like Merrill Lynch, PaineWebber, or Kemper.

Load Versus No-Load Funds

There are two basic kinds of mutual funds, differentiated by the method by which they are sold. When you pay a commission to a salesperson, financial planner, or broker, that fee is called a *load*. One kind of fund therefore is called a *load mutual fund* because you have to pay a commission to buy it. The other kind of fund, called a *no-load fund*, is sold directly by the mutual fund company, with no salesperson involved. To buy no-load shares, you call the mutual fund company directly, usually at a toll-free 800 number, and it sends you the necessary prospectus and application forms. Sending them back with a check opens your account..

Both load and no-load funds have their roles in the marketplace, and you must decide which is best for your needs. The advantage of a load fund is that you receive professional advice on which fund to choose. Such advice may be well worthwhile because it might be difficult for you to isolate the few funds that are best for your situation among the more than 4,000 funds in existence. Ideally, the salesperson helping you will not only tell you when to buy the fund but also when to sell your shares and move your money into a better fund.

The disadvantage of a load fund is that the commission you must pay immediately reduces the amount of money you have at work in the fund. The load can amount to as much as 8.5 percent of your initial investment, though many funds today charge 3 percent or 4 percent. Thus, for every dollar you sink into the fund, only 91.5 cents will earn money if you pay the full 8.5 percent load. If you pay a 3 percent load, 97 cents of every dollar will be invested in stocks. In the short term, therefore, you are starting at a disadvantage over a no-load fund, where all of your dollar is at work from the beginning. Over a longer time period, however, if the load fund performs better than the no-load fund, the up-front charge will pale in significance.

Clearly, the advantage of the no-load fund is that you have all of your money working for you from the moment you open your account. The disadvantage of a no-load fund is that you will not receive much, if any, guidance on which fund to buy. When you call a no-load company's toll-free number, the phone representative can explain the differences between all of the firm's offerings. He or she can describe each fund's investment objective, track record, dividend yield, size in assets, management style and fees, and the stocks currently in its portfolio. But because the person does not know you or your situation, and chances are will never speak to you again, he or she cannot advise you on which fund to buy. If you already have made up your mind based on information you have received about the fund from the fund company itself or reports in the press, that may be no problem. Just realize that you are taking full responsibility for your investment decisions when you buy a no-load fund. No salesperson will call to sell you more of the fund, and no one will tell you when to sell your shares and move to a better performing fund.

People often wonder how no-load companies can offer mutual funds if they do not charge for the service. In fact, they charge plenty, but it is not in the form of an explicit fee for which you must write a check. Both no-load and load funds levy what is known as a *management fee* every year to compensate them for the services they render. The management fee, which ranges from as little as

.2 percent of your assets to as much as 2 percent, is deducted from the value of the fund automatically. So, if a fund charges a 1 percent management fee, for example, and the fund's stock portfolio rose 10 percent over the last year, you will earn a 9 percent return. As long as you keep your money in a fund, you will pay the management fee, though you might never realize it. A management fee, listed in a fund's selling literature as part of the expense ratio, should not be much more than 1.25 percent of its (and therefore your) assets for it to be considered fair and reasonable.

The Advantages of Mutual Funds

Mutual funds offer several key advantages over individual stocks, which can make the management fee very worthwhile.

A professional skilled in choosing stocks does all of your work for you. Managers of stock mutual funds spend their entire day determining which stocks to buy and sell. They have instant access to information about every stock around the world at the push of a few computer keys. They work in companies where teams of research analysts pore over corporate quarterly and annual reports, and managers and analysts visit company executives and factories to evaluate the firms' prospects firsthand. You have almost no opportunity to become as knowledgeable as these fund managers without quitting your job and taking up investing full time.

A mutual fund gives you instant diversification. If you have only $1,000 or $5,000 to invest, the money will not buy many shares of a single stock, and it will certainly not buy many different stocks. By putting your money in only two or three stocks, you are exposed to the possibility that one of them will plummet in price, wiping out much of your investment capital. Instead, when you put your $1,000 or $5,000 in a mutual fund, your money buys into a portfolio that may comprise 50 stocks, or maybe 500 different issues. If one or two stocks in the portfolio get hit hard, your losses will be much more limited because many of the other stocks will probably be going up at the same time.

A fund exists for every financial goal and risk tolerance level. Depending on your goals and risk level, you can find a fund that fits your situation. The different types of funds are described in more detail later in this chapter, but in broad terms, there are funds designed for various degrees of growth and for varying levels of income, as well as funds that combine both growth and income objectives.

Transaction costs are much lower. When you invest in a mutual fund, you benefit from the brokerage commission rates paid by the fund company, which are far lower than you would pay to make the same trades. Mutual funds are among the largest institutional investors on Wall Street, and because they buy and sell billions of dollars' worth of stock every day, they pay between $.02 and $.05 a share per trade. You would be lucky to pay $.10 a share at most brokerage firms, and if you trade in quantities of less than $1,000, you might have to pay as much as $.40 or $.50 a share. Over time, the lower transaction costs that the mutual fund pays will boost your return because you will have more money invested and less paid out in fees.

You can get into and out of a mutual fund easily. All it takes is a phone call to your broker or the fund. By law, a fund must allow you to buy shares at the fund's closing price on the day the fund gets your money. The closing price, called *net asset value* (NAV), is the value of the stock portfolio at the end of the day divided by the number of shares in the fund. Conversely, if you want to sell, the fund must redeem your shares at the NAV on the day you give your instructions. This instant liquidity can be a big advantage when you want to buy or sell stocks quickly. For example, say stock prices are shooting up and you still haven't determined which stocks to buy, or you can't get your broker on the phone. Instead of watching helplessly on the sidelines, you can participate in the rally by buying a stock fund. On the other hand, if stock prices are plunging, it may be difficult to get decent prices if you have only a handful of shares to sell. When you sell the mutual fund, you know you will receive the fund's closing price that day, no matter what problems the fund manager has selling stocks.

In addition to buying and selling fund shares on your request, mutual funds can set up automatic systems to add or subtract money from your account. Most mutual funds will automatically transfer a set amount – usually as little as $25 – from your bank account or money-market mutual fund into the stock or bond fund of your choice on a regular basis, whether that be weekly, monthly, or annually. Many mutual funds actually waive their normal initial minimum investment amount of $1,000 if you sign up for such a plan. This is a simple way to invest on autopilot. You probably won't even miss the money from your checking account, but over time, you will build up your capital in the mutual fund. On the other hand, if you are retired and want a regular income, most mutual funds will automatically withdraw a certain amount of money and send you a monthly check. This is called an *automatic withdrawal program*, and it allows you to withdraw a regular amount of money from your funds every month. It is targeted mostly to retired people living off their funds.

You can easily switch from one fund to another within a fund family. Most mutual fund companies offer a broad array of mutual funds so that as your views of the stock market or your needs change, you can simply switch from one fund to another. This is known as an *exchange.* For instance, you may

Fig. ⑪ The Effect of Compounding on a Berger 100 Fund Investment

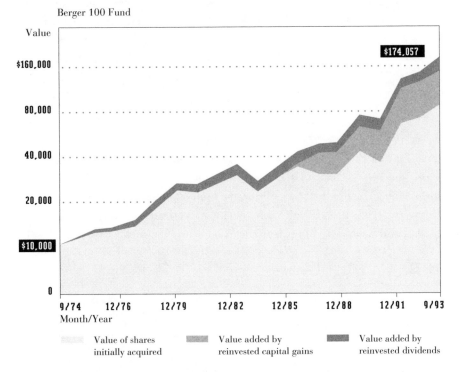

Berger 100 Fund

$174,057

| Value of shares initially acquired | Value added by reinvested capital gains | Value added by reinvested dividends |

Source: Adapted and used by permission of Berger Associates and Tower Data Systems.
Past performance shows the fund's history and does not guarantee future results. The figures include changes in share price and reinvestment of dividends and capital gains, which will fluctuate so that shares, when redeemed, may be worth more or less than their original cost. The figures include the deduction of 12b-1 fees beginning in June 1990.

have invested money in a growth stock fund for years to build capital for retirement. When you retire, you can exchange some of the shares in the growth fund for shares in a stock fund paying high dividends on a monthly basis, on which you will live. All fund families allow exchanges not only between stock funds but also from stock funds to bond funds and money-market funds, which may act as havens when stock prices are falling.

The fund will reinvest dividends and capital gains automatically. If you want the power of compounding to work for you, you can instruct your mutual fund to reinvest in more fund shares all dividends it has earned from the stocks in its portfolio. In addition, as the fund captures capital gains by selling stocks at a profit, it disburses the proceeds as capital gains distributions. You can have the fund reinvest those distributions in more shares as well. Remember to pay taxes on both reinvested dividends and capital gains in the tax year you receive them, even though you have reinvested the money.

Over time, the shares you own from reinvestment produce more shares, and the compounding effect can dramatically increase your capital. For example, if you invested $10,000 in the Denver-based Berger 100 Fund on September 30, 1974, you would have accumulated $174,057 by September 30, 1993, assuming you had reinvested all dividends and capital gains distributions. In contrast, your $10,000 would have grown to only $86,598 if you had taken the distributions. The graph in Figure 11 clearly illustrates the power of compounding.

More on Fund Fees

Some mutual funds levy additional charges, which you should be aware of before you invest. The funds cannot sneak these charges by you. They are all disclosed in a standardized fee table on the front of all mutual fund prospectuses. *Prospectuses* are the official legal documents describing funds. The section, titled "Fund Expenses," appears in the example in Figure 12.

Fig. 12 Charges That Funds Levy

Fund Expenses
The following table sets forth the fees that an investor in the Fund might pay and expenses paid by the Fund during its fiscal year ended December 31, 1991.

Shareholder Transaction Expenses

Maximum Sales Charge on Purchases (as a percentage of offering price)	5.75%
Sales Charge on Reinvested Dividends	None
Redemption Fee	None
Deferred Sales Load	None*
Exchange Fee	$5.00

Annual Fund Operating Expenses
(as a percentage of average net assets)

Management Fees	.65%
12b-1 (Distribution Plan) Fees	.08%
Other Expenses	22%
Total Fund Operating Expenses	.95%

The following example applies the above-stated expenses to a hypothetical $1,000 investment in shares of the Fund over the time periods shown below, assuming a 5% annual rate of return on the investment and also assuming that the shares were redeemed at the end of each stated period. The amounts below are the cumulative costs of such hypothetical $1,000 investment for the periods shown.

1 year	3 years	5 years	10 years
$67	$86	$107	$167

This example should not be considered a representation of past or future expenses or performance. Expenses are subject to change and actual performance and expenses may be less or greater than those illustrated above. For further details, see the Fund's Financial Statements included in the Additional Statement.

*Certain purchases of $1 million or more are not subject to front-end sales charges but a contingent deferred sales charge of 1% is imposed on the proceeds of such shares redeemed within 18 months of the end of the calendar month of their purchase, subject to certain conditions. See "How to Buy Shares – Contingent Deferred Sales Charge," below.

The purpose of this table is to assist an investor in understanding the various costs and expenses that an investor in the Fund will bear directly (shareholder transaction expenses) or indirectly (annual fund operating expenses). The sales charge illustrated is the current maximum rate applicable to purchases of Fund shares. Investors may be entitled to reduced sales charges based on the amount purchased or the value of shares already owned and may be subject to a contingent deferred sales charge in limited circumstances (see "How to Buy Shares"). "Other Expenses" includes such expenses as custodial and transfer agent fees, audit, legal and other business operating expenses, but excludes extraordinary expenses.

Source: Adapted with permission of OppenheimerFunds.SM

Note that funds are required to detail their expenses by category for the last year. In addition, they must project what that level of expenses would cost investors if they invested $1,000 over the next year, three years, five years, and 10 years. You can use this section of the prospectus to compare one mutual fund with a similar fund in another fund family.

An explanation of the most common fund fees follows.

Back-end loads.

To compete with no-load funds, many broker-sold funds now waive a charge when you buy them but hit you with a fee if you sell the funds before a particular period of time elapses. This is also called a *contingent deferred sales charge.* Usually, the back-end load operates on a sliding scale, so you will pay 4 percent of the money you invested if you sell the fund in the first year you hold it, 3 percent in the second year, 2 percent in the third year, and 1 percent in the fourth year. If you hold the fund for at least four years, you will not pay the back-end load. A brokerage firm needs this system because it pays the broker his or her commission up front when you buy the fund, even though the firm doesn't receive the money from you to pay the commission. If you sell the fund before the brokerage firm has had a chance to recoup that fee through management fees, it wants to be able to charge you.

12b-1 fees.

These charges, like management fees, are deducted automatically from the fund's assets each year. They cover distribution costs, which include advertising, promotion, literature, and sales incentives to brokers, and range from .25 percent to as much as 1.25 percent of the fund's assets each year. The idea behind these fees is that if a mutual fund increases its assets through more promotion, fund shareholders will benefit because the fund's expenses will be spread over a wider customer base, thereby lowering each shareholder's cost. In many cases, however, expenses do not decrease as fund assets grow. In general, unless you invest in a fund that has a superb record or some other compelling reason to buy it, avoid funds that impose 12b-1 fees.

[**Buying Shares in a Stock Mutual Fund**]

The Prospectus

Mutual fund companies have made it as easy as possible to open an account, but there is still a certain amount of legal paperwork you must go through in the process. In protecting consumers and making sure they receive enough information about a fund, the Securities and Exchange Commission (SEC) requires that potential fund shareholders receive a prospectus and an application form from the fund. While you shouldn't expect the prospectus to compete with your favorite novel for light reading, it does contain several important facts you should understand before you give the fund any money. The following are the most important areas the prospectus covers.

• *The fund's investment objective.* It may be aiming for aggressive growth, steady income, or something in between.

• *The investment methods the fund uses to achieve its goals.* It may restrict itself to certain kinds of stocks, or it may use complex hedging strategies involving futures and options to prevent losses. The fund will also tell you what kinds of stocks it will not buy.

• *The fund's investment adviser.* The prospectus will outline the background of the fund company and usually tell you which portfolio manager makes the decisions about what stocks to buy and sell. Ultimately, the fund's performance is determined by the quality of the investment adviser. Some firms use a team approach, while others are run by an individual who decides what to buy or sell.

• *The amount of risk the fund will assume.* Depending on the type of fund, the prospectus will reveal how volatile the fund's price is. The more risks the fund takes, the more its price will jump around.

• *The tax consequences of holding the fund.* For example, the prospectus will mention that you must pay taxes on all dividend and capital gains distributions.

• *A list of services provided by the fund.* The prospectus will tell you whether the fund is suitable for individual retirement accounts (IRAs) and Keogh accounts, whether you can reinvest dividends and capital gains automatically, and whether you can set up an automatic investment or withdrawal program. The prospectus will also tell you the minimum initial investment to get into the fund, as well as the minimum amount to make subsequent investments.

• *A financial summary of the fund's performance for the last 10 years, if it has been around that long.* A table will track the fund's price, dividends and capital gains distributions that have been paid, and expenses.

• *A listing of all fund fees.* This table will summarize the management fee, 12b-1 fees, sales charges, and any other fees charged to shareholders.

As with all investments, before you sink your money into any fund, you should review your financial goals and your risk tolerance level. Also, you should place each fund you consider at its appropriate level in the investment pyramid.

The following is a rundown of the different categories of stock funds, separated into the sectors of the investment pyramid.

High-Risk Apex Funds

Aggressive growth funds.
These funds buy stocks of fast-growing companies or of other companies that have great capital gains potential. Or they might buy stocks in bankrupt or depressed companies, anticipating a rebound. Such funds often trade stocks frequently in hope of catching small price gains. They are also known as maximum capital gains funds.

Foreign stock funds.
These funds buy stocks of corporations based outside of the United States. In addition to the usual forces affecting stock prices, fluctuations in the value of the U.S. dollar against foreign currencies can dramatically affect the price of these funds' shares, particularly over the short term.

Sector funds.
Sector funds buy stocks in just one industry or sector of the economy. Some examples would be environmental stocks, oil company shares and stocks in automakers and gold-mining companies. Because these funds are undiversified, they soar or plummet on the fate of the industry in which they invest.

Small-company growth funds.
Such growth funds invest in stocks of small companies, typically those having outstanding shares with a total market value of $500 million or less. These companies have enormous growth potential, yet the stocks they invest in are much less established – and therefore riskier – than blue chip stocks.

Special situation funds.
These funds often place large bets on a small number of stocks, anticipating a big payoff. The "special situation" the fund manager looks for might be a takeover or a liquidation of the company at a price higher than the shares currently sell for. Some funds offer venture capital financing for privately held firms, hoping to cash in when the companies offer shares to the public in the future.

Moderate-Risk Sector Funds

Growth funds.

Growth funds invest in shares of well-known growth companies that usually have a long history of increasing earnings. Because the stock market fluctuates, growth funds rise and fall over time as well, though not as much as funds holding smaller, less proven stocks.

Equity-income funds.

Such funds own shares in stocks that pay higher dividends than do growth funds. Whereas a growth fund's payout may be 1 percent or 2 percent, an equity-income fund might yield 4 percent or 5 percent. That higher yield tends to cushion the fund's price when stock prices fall. When stock prices rise, equity-income funds tend to increase less sharply than do pure growth funds. A slightly more aggressive version of an equity-income fund is called a *growth and income fund* or a *total return fund* because it strives for gains from both income and capital appreciation.

Index funds.

These funds buy the stocks that make up a particular index to allow investors' returns to match the index. The most popular index used is the Standard & Poor's 500. Proponents of index funds argue that because many money managers fail to match or beat the S&P 500 each year, investors can come out ahead by just matching the index. The management fees of an index fund are much lower than those of a regular stock fund because the fund manager just replicates an index; he or she does not research or make decisions on which stocks to buy and sell.

Option-income funds.

These funds buy stocks and write options on the shares, which generates more income for shareholders. This usually results in a higher dividend than growth funds offer. On the other hand, if stock prices rise, the funds lose their position in the stocks because the options are exercised. Therefore, these funds have limited appreciation potential.

Socially conscious funds.

Such funds look for companies that meet certain criteria, such as advancing minority and women employees or helping clean up the environment. These funds screen out stocks of companies that are major polluters, defense contractors or promoters of gambling or tobacco.

Low-Risk Sector Funds

Balanced funds.

Balanced funds keep a fairly steady mix of high-yielding stocks and conservative bonds. This allows the funds to pay a fairly high rate of current income and still participate in the long-term growth of stocks.

Flexible portfolio funds.

These funds have the latitude to invest in stocks, bonds, or cash instruments, depending on the fund manager's market outlook. If he or she thinks stock prices are about to fall, the manager can shift all the fund's assets into cash instruments, thereby avoiding losses. If he or she thinks stock prices are about to rise, the manager can move all the fund's assets into stocks. Usually, the fund will have some money in stocks, bonds, and cash, which tends to stabilize its performance. These funds are also known as *asset allocation funds.*

Utilities funds.

Such funds buy shares in electric, gas, telephone, and water utilities. Because all these companies are regulated monopolies, they have steady earnings and pay high dividends. Utilities funds are subject to swings in interest rates, however. Nonetheless, for a high-yielding and relatively stable stock fund, it's hard to beat a utilities fund.

Another way to look at this trade-off between risk and return is illustrated in the dial in Figure 13.

Fig. 13 Trading Risk for Return: A Mutual Fund Dial

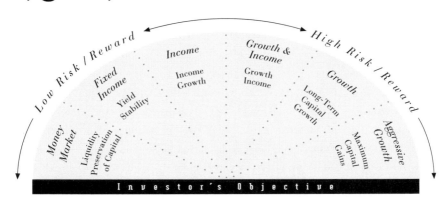

Source: Adapted from *The Investor's Guide to Low-Cost Mutual Funds.* Reprinted by permission of The Mutual Fund Education Alliance.

Selecting a Fund Within a Category

Once you have chosen the fund category that fits your needs, you must narrow your options further by looking at the best funds within the category.

Performance.

The first criterion in selecting a particular fund is performance. You want to choose a fund that has established a solid long-term record of achieving its objectives. It is also preferable if the fund has had the same manager for a long time so that you can be assured that the fund's style will remain consistent.

Several independent fund-monitoring organizations rank fund performance. The two biggest and best known are Lipper Analytical Services (74 Trinity Pl., New York, NY 10006; 212-393-1300) and Morningstar (53 W. Jackson Blvd., Chicago, IL 60604; 800-876-5005). Results from both are published regularly in *The Wall Street Journal, USA Today,* and *Investor's Business Daily,* as well as MONEY Magazine. You can also track fund performance in the many newsletters that follow this action.

The best measure of fund performance is called *total return.* This combines all dividends and capital gains distributions with changes in a fund's price. It is a far better yardstick to use when comparing funds than just the change in a fund's price over a period of time. The listings for total return you will see from the ratings services and in the media normally show a fund's results thus far in the current year, over the last 52 weeks and over the last three, five, and 10 years. They will also refer to the *average annual return,* which is the averaging of returns over longer periods of time. Any average annual return of more than 15 percent for at least five years is considered exemplary.

In choosing a fund, you should feel comfortable with its *style.* What exactly *is* a fund's style? It is a methodology of selecting stocks that differentiates one fund from another. Some styles work well at certain points in a stock market cycle, while others take over as the stock market changes. The two broadest kinds of stock-choosing styles are growth and value. *Growth* refers to selecting stocks with ever-rising earnings, while *value* means buying stocks temporarily out of favor that the manager expects will become popular again. Therefore, you can often determine a fund's style by its name. For instance, the Kemper Growth Fund is a classic growth stock fund, while the T. Rowe Price Small-Cap Value Fund looks for small stocks that are currently out of favor. In general, growth stocks shine when the economy is well into an economic recovery, while value stocks tend to outperform others when the economy is in recession or is just starting to emerge from a recession.

It is difficult for the average investor, as well as the Wall Street professional, to evaluate whether growth or value stock funds are on the upswing at any particular moment. For that reason, the best long-term strategy is to diversify among styles. If half your holdings are in growth stocks and the other half are in value stocks, you will perform better over time than if you invest all your money in one style of stock.

Another difference in investment styles is based on whether the fund manager makes *market timing* decisions. A fund run by a market timer, even though it is a stock fund, can sell most or all of its stocks if the manager senses the stock market is about to tumble. This fund is designed to protect shareholders' capital from huge losses. Funds operating under the other style maintain that it is impossible to time the stock market's ups and downs, so it is best to be nearly fully invested in stocks at all times. These funds will be more volatile than funds that try to time the market. This means that fully invested funds will rise faster when stocks rise but fall further when stocks tumble. The managers of such funds leave the market timing to you.

Convenience.

The second criterion you should use to choose a fund is convenience. Though you might receive a higher return by having holdings in the top 10 funds in 10 different fund families, the recordkeeping and headaches in following so many funds are most likely not worth the higher return. It's probably best to find a top-quality fund family or two and keep most of your capital with them. Most families offer consolidated statements, meaning you can see all of your fund holdings on one statement. Also, you will be able to transfer money from one fund to another easily if you keep most of your assets in one place.

You have one way around this problem of proliferating fund families. Several discount brokers, including Charles Schwab, Fidelity, and Jack White, allow you to buy almost any mutual fund in any family and keep it in one account. Schwab calls its service the Mutual Fund Marketplace or OneSource; Fidelity calls its equivalent FundsNetwork. For many funds, you pay no loads, transaction fees, or commissions. By consolidating all of your fund holdings under one custodian, you can save yourself much frustration and still participate in the best funds.

Quality of service.

The quality of the service you receive is also important in choosing a fund family. While most fund complexes offer good service, there are variations. Following are a few services that top fund groups offer. You should have access to each of them.

• *Automated phone answering systems* that can give you prices, yields, and other information about your funds, as well as allow you to make transactions. In many cases, these systems operate 24 hours a day, seven days a week.

• *Knowledgeable and helpful telephone service representatives.* Remember that phone reps at no-load funds will describe funds but will not advise you on which fund to buy. Some large fund companies have walk-in investor centers in large cities where you can discuss your investing needs with a fund representative in person.

• *Easy-to-read statements.* You should not have to be a lawyer or mutual fund expert to be able to make sense of your statement. It should clearly spell out how many shares you have, how many shares you bought or sold in your latest transactions, the yields on your funds, and other relevant data. Most funds will calculate your *cost basis*, which is the amount of money you spent to buy your shares. That can be quite complex to ascertain on your own if you have been buying shares with reinvested dividends and capital gains for years. You will need your cost basis to determine the amount of taxes you owe when you sell fund shares.

Once you have opened an account with a fund that meets your criteria, hold onto it unless its performance starts to deteriorate, its fees shoot up, its star manager leaves, its style changes dramatically, or you have some other major reason to sell the fund. That includes, of course, a change in your financial situation or your stage in the life cycle. Otherwise, continue to add to the fund and watch it grow!

[Closed-End Mutual Funds]

So far, all of our discussion of mutual funds has pertained to open-end funds. Another variety of fund is called a *closed-end fund*, which has its own advantages and disadvantages.

Like open-end funds, closed-end funds offer the advantages of professional management, diversification, convenience, and automatic reinvestment of dividends and capital gains.

The difference between the two types of funds comes in the way they sell shares. Open-end funds create new shares continually, as more money is invested in them. When cash is taken out of the fund, the number of outstanding shares shrinks. The portfolio manager therefore is faced with an ever-changing pool of assets that can be small one month and huge the next. This can make it difficult to manage the fund because millions of dollars usually pour into the fund after it has had a hot record and stock prices are high, and millions leave the fund when it has underperformed the market and stock prices are falling. This pattern of volatile cash flow can severely harm the fund's performance because the manager is forced to buy stocks when prices are high and sell them when prices are low.

Closed-end funds are designed to avoid this problem. Instead of constantly creating and redeeming shares, these funds issue a limited number of shares, which trade on the New York or American Stock Exchange or on the Nasdaq National Market System. Instead of dealing with the fund company directly when you buy or sell shares, as you do with open-end funds, you trade closed-end shares with other investors, just as you do any publicly traded stock. You pay standard brokerage commissions to buy and sell them, and you can look up the fund's price in the stock tables of the newspaper every day.

From the closed-end fund manager's point of view, there is no need to worry about huge flows of cash into and out of the fund. The manager knows how much money he or she must invest and selects stocks based on the fund's investment objective. This allows the manager to concentrate on meeting long-term objectives because he or she does not have to keep a stash of cash around to meet redemptions.

Like an open-end fund, a closed-end fund always has a certain NAV (*net asset value*, the worth of all the stocks in its portfolio divided by the number of shares). But unlike an open-end fund, a closed-ender can sell for more or less than the value of its portfolio, depending on demand for the shares.

When the fund sells for more than its portfolio is currently worth, that is called *selling at a premium*. This usually happens when the fund is extremely popular and it offers some unique style or investing niche, which makes investors willing to pay a high price for it. For example, the Korea Fund, which was the only fund granted permission to invest in fast-growing Korea by the Korean government, soared to a 100 percent premium at one point because investors had no other way of investing in Korea. That means that investors were willing to pay $20 a share – or double the $10 that the underlying portfolio of Korean stocks was worth. Another reason a fund might sell at a premium is that it is named after a famous money manager with a good track record, so brokers actively sell it. Funds that meet this description include the Gabelli Fund, the Templeton Emerging Markets Fund, and the Zweig Fund.

In general, closed-end funds tend to jump to premiums immediately after they first issue shares to the public because the brokerage firms that underwrite the issues actively promote them for a few months. Often, once the brokers have moved on to the next closed-end issue, the older funds drop to a discount. The moral of the story: It almost never pays to buy a new issue of a closed-end fund.

On the other hand, a fund investing in an unpopular category of stocks can fall to a steep discount. For example, the Brazil Fund dropped to a 35 percent discount when the country was suffering through a bout of political scandals and hyperinflation. That means a buyer paid only $6.50 per share, or 65 percent of the $10 value of the Brazilian stock portfolio. Closed-end funds can also drop to discounts because few people pay attention to them and therefore there is little demand for them. That can provide an opportunity to buy assets cheaply. In fact, if a fund's discount remains too deep for too long a time, raiders will often swoop in. Their game is to buy millions of shares at a discount, then force a vote to convert the fund from closed-end to open-end status. Because open-end funds always trade at the worth of their underlying portfolios, the raiders can walk off with huge profits.

Therefore, you should assess two factors when you buy a closed-end fund. The first is the fund manager's record in choosing winning stocks that allow the fund to achieve its investment objective. The second factor is whether you are buying the fund at a premium or a discount. Some investors' entire strategy with closed-end funds is to buy them at a discount and wait for them to rise to a premium, at which point they sell.

To determine whether a fund is selling at a premium or a discount, you can look in Monday's *Wall Street Journal* in the "Money and Investing" section or in *Barron's*. A sample table, along with an explanation of each column, follows.

Fund [1]	Stock Exchange [2]	Net Asset Value [3]	Stock Price [4]	% Difference [5]
Baker Fentress Fund	AMEX	$9.00	$10.00	+11%
China Fund	NYSE	$13.00	$10.00	−23%

1. Column 1 lists the name of the fund. Funds are broken down alphabetically by categories, such as diversified funds, specialized equity funds and bond funds.
2. The second column notes the exchange where the fund's shares are traded. In the example, Baker Fentress shares trade on the American Stock Exchange, and the China Fund trades on the New York Stock Exchange.
3. The *NAV* is the total per-share worth of the underlying portfolio of securities on this day. In the example, all of the stocks in the Baker Fentress Fund, divided by the number of fund shares, are worth $9 per mutual fund share.
4. The *stock price* is the dollar amount that the fund currently sells for on the New York or American Stock Exchange.
5. The *difference* is the percentage difference between the stock price and the NAV. In the example, the Baker Fentress Fund is trading at an 11 percent premium, while the China Fund is selling at a 23 percent discount.

There are several kinds of closed-end funds, each with its own objective and risk characteristics. Some of the most common types follow.

Balanced funds.

Balanced funds buy a mix of stocks and bonds to provide shareholders with both capital appreciation and hefty dividends. They are for conservative investors.

Diversified equity funds.

These funds buy a portfolio of stocks in many industries. If the fund manager is bearish (the manager thinks that the stock prices are about to fall), though, the fund can hold cash or some bonds. The objective of diversified equity funds is usually growth.

Dual-purpose funds.

Such funds require two classes of shares. One class, called *capital shares*, is designed for capital appreciation; and the other, called *income shares*, is designed to provide high current income. Capital shareholders receive all the changes in the value of the fund's portfolio, and income shareholders receive all investment income from dividends and interest.

International funds.

International funds buy stocks in countries around the world. Their prices are therefore affected not only by changes in stock prices but also by fluctuations of foreign currencies against the U.S. dollar. Some international funds specialize in a particular area of the world, like Europe or Asia. Some specialize in stocks of developing countries. Some funds buy stocks in a particular industry, like health care or telecommunications, on a worldwide basis.

Single-country funds.

Such funds invest in the stocks of a single country. This makes them more volatile than broadly diversified international funds. For example, on the euphoria about the possibilities of German reunification, the Germany Fund shot up sharply to a huge premium after the Berlin Wall fell. A few years later, when it was clear that reunification would take longer and be more costly than expected, shares in the Germany Fund fell to a deep discount.

For both beginning and sophisticated investors, there is probably no better way to set up a diversified portfolio than through mutual funds. Both open- and closed-end funds offer many services at reasonable cost. The wide array of choices of different types of funds means that there is a fund for every investing need you may ever have, from the most aggressive to the most conservative. Millions of shareholders who have studied about and invested in funds are satisfied with their holdings. With the explanation of mutual funds provided by this chapter, you should now feel more confident about choosing the best fund for your situation.

[FOUR]

Investing in Bonds

hen you invest in a *bond*, you are loaning the issuer of that bond your money in return for a fixed rate of interest for a specific amount of time. Normally, you receive interest payments every six months, and when the bond matures, you receive your original principal, no matter how much the price of the bond fluctuated since it was issued.

Bonds are one of the key investment vehicles available for your use in achieving your financial goals. They allow you to lock in a set rate of income for a long period of time, which can give your financial plan a rock-solid foundation. In addition, if you want to trade bonds more actively, you can earn capital gains by buying them when their prices fall and selling them when their prices rise, just as you can do with stocks.

[The Basics of Holding Bonds]

When you buy bonds issued by a government agency or a company, you become a lender to that entity. This is very different from being a stockholder, which you become when you buy a company's stock. As a bondholder, you are entitled to receive the bond's stated interest rate when interest is due and your principal when the bond matures – nothing more. You will not receive quarterly or annual reports. You will not be invited to a firm's annual meeting. You will not earn dividends. If a company's earnings soar, you will not participate in that success.

On the other hand, the yield you will receive from the bond will typically be higher than the stock dividend yield because bondholders must be compensated for reduced purchasing power in the future because of inflation. (Of course, there is no way to buy stock in most government agencies – although you can buy stock in some – so bonds are the only way to participate in the government.)

As with stocks, the money that you pay to buy bonds goes to the issuers only when the bonds are first sold to the public. After that, you buy bonds from the existing owners, or you sell bonds to other investors. Most bond trading is done automatically in a computer-driven system without specialists or dealers. In addition, bonds are bought and sold through competing dealers, who communicate with each other by computer and telephone.

Bonds are normally quoted on a price scale of zero to 200, with 100 being the price at which the bond was issued, or what is known as *par*. Because bonds are sold in minimum denominations of $1,000, a price of 100 means that the bond is trading at $1,000 per bond. If the bond's price rises to 110, your holdings are now worth $1,100.

Unlike stock transactions, bond buy-and-sell transactions normally occur without a separate commission charge. Instead, a broker makes money from a transaction by taking a piece of the spread between the buying and selling prices. For example, if a broker buys you a bond at a price of 100, he or she might charge you 102 for it and keep the two points as his or her commission. If you try to sell the bond for a price of 100, you might get only 98 for it. Because the bond market is generally dominated by large institutions that trade millions of dollars' worth of bonds, you will pay a wider spread if you buy only a small number of bonds. Many bond dealers won't even execute a trade for fewer than 25 bonds, or $25,000, though some might go as low as five bonds, or $5,000. Because it is a competitive market, you should shop around among brokers to get the best deal.

The only way you can avoid paying a large spread for small purchases, other than to buy bonds through a mutual fund, is to buy government bonds directly from the Treasury. You can buy bills, notes, and bonds whenever the Treasury auctions new issues. You can also buy U.S. savings bonds for only $25 through any bank or by payroll deduction. (Government bonds will be discussed in more detail later.)

For decades, bondholders received fancy bond certificates with attached coupons entitling the coupon owners to the cash interest payment on the date due. These were known as *bearer bonds* because whoever bore a bond coupon would be paid the interest. Bearer bonds have not been issued since 1982; therefore, for the most part, the days of bearer bond certificates are long gone. Instead, bonds are now issued in either *registered* or *book entry form*. Registered bonds still have certificates, and the owner of the bond is named on the back of the certificate. To sell a registered bond, the owner must endorse it and have his or her name changed to the new owner's name in the issuer's records. The more common form of bond issued today, however, is the *book entry bond*, for which interest payments are tracked by computers. If you hold a bond in a brokerage account, interest and principal payments will be made automatically. Book entry bonds provide no certificate you can hold in your hands; the record exists only in the computer data banks of your brokerage firm. Because the bond is electronic, however, it is much easier to trade because no endorsement is needed for the bond to change hands.

How Bond Prices Move

When you consider investing in bonds, you should understand that one cardinal rule about the movement of bond prices: *Bond prices move in the opposite direction of interest rates.* Normally, you might think that rising interest rates would be good for your bond, but nothing could be further from the truth. Even though it may sound illogical at first, it is true that when interest rates rise, bond prices fall. When interest rates fall, bond prices rise. The following example explains why.

Say you buy a bond yielding 10 percent at a price of 100 (the par price). If interest rates plummet to 5 percent over the next several years, your 10 percent bond would become very valuable, indeed. Its price would soar – maybe to a dollar value of 150 – because people would be willing to pay a big premium to get their hands on a 10 percent bond in an environment where bonds pay only 5 percent. Notice that as interest rates fell, your bond's value rose.

Now let's take the opposite situation. You buy your 10 percent bond at 100, and instead of dropping, interest rates soar to 15 percent. Your bond won't be popular now because people would rather buy a new bond paying 15 percent than your old bond paying 10 percent. Therefore, if you want to sell your bond to buy a newer one at the higher current rate, you would suffer a loss. The price of your bond might drop to half, from 100 to 50. Notice that as interest rates rose, your bond's value fell.

Bond prices move so perversely because bonds are a fixed-rate instrument. Because the bond's rate is locked in at whatever level it was when the bond was first issued, the bond becomes more or less valuable as interest rates fall or rise. Figure 14 might help you better understand the inverse relationship between interest rates and bond prices.

The longer the maturity of your bond, the more its price will react to the ups and downs of interest rates. A bond that locks in a high interest rate for 20 or 30 years is much more valuable to an investor if interest rates have fallen than a bond that matures in a year or two. Conversely, if interest rates have risen, the investor would rather get his or her money back quickly so he or she can reinvest at higher rates.

Fig. **14** Relationship Between Bond Funds and Interest Rates

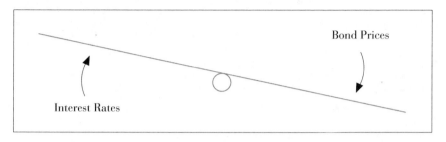

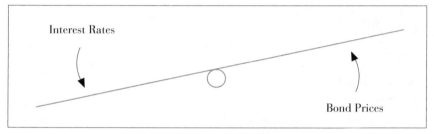

Short-term bonds (bonds that are close to maturity) are usually less affected by changes in interest rates than long-term bonds.

When calculating the effect of interest rates on an investor's holdings, analysts usually look at the total return – that is, the price change of the bond added to the income it is paying. Figure 15 shows how an interest rate increase of from one to four percentage points over one year would affect the total returns of several bond maturities, from six years to 30 years. This table assumes that six-year bonds yield 6 percent, 10- and 20-year bonds yield 7 percent and 30-year bonds yield 8 percent. Notice that the longer the bond maturity, the more the bond loses value as rates rise.

Figure 16 shows how much total returns on different bond maturities rise as interest rates fall over one year.

Fig. **15** Percentage Points Rate Increase in a Year

Maturity	Unchanged	+1%	+2%	+3%	+4%
6 Years	+6%	+2%	−2%	− 5%	− 9%
10 Years	+7	+1	−5	−10	−15
20 Years	+7	+1	−7	−13	−19
30 Years	+8	−3	−11	−19	−25

Source: Reprinted by permission of The Leuthold Group, an investment advisory firm in Minneapolis, Minnesota.

Fig. **16** Percentage Points Rate Decrease in a Year

Maturity	Unchanged	-1%	-2%	-3%	-4%
6 Years	+6%	+10%	+15%	+20%	+25%
10 Years	+7	+13	+20	+28	+37
20 Years	+7	+18	+28	+42	+57
30 Years	+8	+20	+35	+51	+69

Source: Reprinted by permission of The Leuthold Group, an investment advisory firm in Minneapolis, Minnesota.

This bond volatility should always factor into your decision to buy bonds.

Why Interest Rates Fluctuate

Many factors influence interest rate movements. In the long term, the outlook for inflation is the most important determinant of interest rates. If inflation is high and rising, investors demand a higher yield to protect the value of their money from erosion. If inflation is low and declining, investors settle for a lower yield because they are not as threatened by the loss of purchasing power. One way to measure investors' fear of inflation is to subtract the current inflation rate from a bond's yield. This produces what is known as the *real interest rate*. For example:

Current interest rate	10%
Consumer price index inflation rate	− 6%
Real interest rate	+ 4%

If the resulting number is positive, it is known as a *positive real interest rate*. In the example, bondholders receive four percentage points more than the current inflation rate. Historically, positive real rates usually average around 3 percent, but they have stretched to 5 percent or 6 percent at times.

If bond rates are lower than inflation, it is known as a *negative interest rate*. For example:

Current interest rate	10%
Consumer price index inflation rate	−13%
Real interest rate	− 3%

In the example, a likely scenario during the late 1970s, bond investors actually lose money because their 10 percent rate is adjusted for rampant inflation.

Because the 1970s lesson was so painful to bond investors, real interest rates have stayed positive since then and are likely to continue to do so because investors want a protective cushion over the current inflation rate. Still, there is no guarantee that yields won't shoot up sharply again in the future and investors will be stuck earning negative real interest rates again.

In addition to the outlook for inflation, supply and demand influence interest rates. If you think of an interest rate as the price of money, you will understand that as demand for money increases and supply decreases, the price, or interest rate, goes up. This situation might occur when the economy is picking up and businesses and consumers want to borrow money to expand and spend, while lenders – including banks and bond buyers – are reluctant to lend because they fear higher interest rates.

Interest rates tend to fall when the economy is declining or in recession because there is little demand for borrowing; businesses are retrenching, and consumers are more interested in paying off existing debts than in taking on new loans. At the same time, a larger supply of money is available to lend because bond buyers want to lock in high interest rates.

Over the last two decades, a new factor has grown in influence on the interest rate level: the federal budget deficit. When the difference between what the government received in taxes and what it spent for programs each year was modest – less than $50 billion – the deficit was easy to cover with national savings. But as the size of the annual deficit grew – first to $100 billion, then to $200 billion, then to a staggering $300 billion – the government consumed more and more of the supply of capital available in the United States. This enormous demand for money by the government as it sells billions of dollars' worth of new bonds, compounded by the fear of an ever-rising national debt, has kept interest rates much higher than they normally would have been if the deficit had been controlled.

While these broad factors influence the general level of interest rates, more specific supply and demand issues affect the interest rates and prices of individual bonds. Whether a bond is issued by a corporation or a municipal agency, investors evaluate it by the strength of its financial condition. The better its financial shape, the more confident investors are that their interest and principal will be repaid on time and, therefore, the lower the bond's interest rate will be. One major factor influencing investors' perceptions of the bond is the rating it receives from one of the three big bond-rating agencies: Standard & Poor's, Moody's and Fitch. Analysts at these agencies, using detailed financial information and judgment based on years of experience, assign a rating to each bond issuer. The ratings scales of the three services appear in Figure 17.

In addition to regular letter grades, Fitch and Standard & Poor's modify ratings with + or – signs. A corporate bond may be rated AA– or BBB+, for instance. Moody's uses numbers from one to three to signify gradations. The same corporate bonds might have a Moody's rating of Aa2 or Baa1, for example.

Fig. ⑰ Bond Rating Services' Rating Systems

	Rating Service		
Explanation of Bond Rating	Standard & Poor's	Moody's	Fitch
Highest quality	AAA	Aaa	AAA
High quality	AA	Aa	AA
Upper medium grade	A	A	A
Medium grade	BBB	Baa	BBB
Predominantly speculative	BB	Ba	BB
Speculative, low grade	B	B	B
Poor to default	CCC	Caa	CCC
Highest speculation	CC	Ca	CC
Lowest quality, not paying interest	C	C	C
In default, in arrears, of questionable value	D		DDD
			DD
			D

Source: Reprinted by permission of Standard & Poor's Corporation, Moody's Investors Service, and Fitch Investors Service, Inc.

Although ratings agencies do not always agree on the risk of default by a particular issuer, their assessments are usually fairly similar. Therefore, such ratings, as well as the prospect for upgradings or downgradings in those ratings, can significantly affect a bond's interest rate and price.

The Meaning of Yield

While a bond has only one interest rate, there are four ways to calculate its *yield* – that is, your return at the bond's current price. They are as follows:

1. *Coupon rate.* The coupon rate is the interest the bond pays. It may equal the bond's yield when it is trading at its issue price of 100, or its $1,000 face value. A bond with a 10 percent coupon, therefore, would pay $100 a year in interest.

2. *Current yield.* This yield adjusts the bond's coupon rate for the bond's current price to determine what percentage you would receive if you bought the bond at its current price. In the example above, if the bond dropped in price from 100 to 90, for instance, the bond's value would fall from $1,000 to $900. At that price, the current yield would rise to 11.1 percent. Current yield is calculated as follows:

$$\frac{\$100 \text{ Annual interest payment of the bond}}{\$900 \text{ Current market price of the bond}} = 11.1\% \text{ Current yield}$$

Remember that rising interest rates cause bond prices to fall. Therefore, in the example, if the bond's price rose from 100 to 110, the bond's value would rise from $1,000 to $1,100. Current yield is calculated as follows:

$$\frac{\$100 \text{ Annual interest payment of the bond}}{\$1,100 \text{ Current market price of the bond}} = 9.09\% \text{ Current yield}$$

Don't worry about having to calculate the yield of every bond you consider buying. Current yields are displayed on your broker's computer screen and also in any newspaper's bond listings.

3. *Yield to maturity.* This yield takes into account the bond's coupon rate, its current price and the years remaining until the bond matures. It is a more complicated calculation, but your broker should be able to tell you the yield to maturity on any bond you are considering. You can also consult a book with yield-to-maturity tables or figure it using a programmable calculator. If you want only to approximate the yield to maturity, you can use the following calculations. This example will use a bond with a 10 percent coupon (paying $100 a year) trading at a price of 85 (now worth $850) with 10 years before it matures.

First, subtract the current bond value (in this case, $850) from par ($1,000) to arrive at the *discount.*

Par	$1,000
Current bond value	− 850
Discount	$150

Divide the discount ($150) by the number of years remaining until the bond matures (10) to calculate the annual gain in the bond's price as it moves from $850 currently to $1,000 at maturity.

$$\frac{\$150 \text{ Discount}}{10 \text{ Years to maturity}} = \$15 \text{ Annual gain}$$

Combine the annual gain ($15) with the bond's annual interest ($100) to get the bond's yearly total gain.

Annual gain	$15
Annual interest	+ 100
Yearly total gain	$115

Divide the yearly total gain ($115) by the bond's current price ($850) to calculate the yield to maturity.

$$\frac{\$115 \text{ Yearly total gain}}{\$850 \text{ Current price of bond}} = 13.5\% \text{ Yield to maturity}$$

4. *Yield to call.* This is the yield up to the first potential date at which the issuer can *call*, or redeem, the bond – usually several years before the bond is scheduled to mature. You calculate the yield to call exactly the same way you calculate the yield to maturity, except that you replace the number of years to maturity with the number of years to the first call date.

You should always assume that a corporation or municipality will put its shareholders' or constituents' interests ahead of bondholders'. Therefore, if interest rates have fallen sharply from the time the bond was issued to the first date that the bond can be called, you should assume the bond will be redeemed. The yield to call is the most realistic yield you can calculate for a bond because you can never assume the bond will remain outstanding between its first call date and its stated maturity.

Early Redemption

A bond can be redeemed before it is scheduled to mature? That sounds illegal. But it isn't – as long as the issuer's ability to redeem the bond is written into the thick legal document that accompanies the original bond issue. In that document, called the *indenture*, bondholders are guaranteed a certain number of years before which the bond cannot be redeemed. This can be as little as five years or as many as 15 to 20 years, although 10-year call protection is more typical.

When the first date of a potential call arrives, the issuer decides whether it makes more sense to continue to pay interest on the bond or to pay off the bond and issue another one at a lower interest rate. For example, if the bond was issued at 10 percent and rates have dropped to 7 percent over the last few years, the issuer would probably refinance. If rates have dropped only to 9 percent, though, refinancing might not be worthwhile. In many cases, bondholders whose bonds are called before maturity will receive a slight premium over par for the bonds. Therefore, they might receive 102 per bond, or $1,020, at redemption. Otherwise, they would receive only par, or $1,000, per bond.

Whenever you consider buying a bond, find out how many years of call protection you have. The more years you know your bond will pay interest, the better.

The Yield Curve

Because bonds mature at some point in the future, the amount of time between now and that maturity point is key in determining the bond's yield and price. In general, the further off an event will occur, the less sure you are about exactly what will happen in the meantime. You might have a pretty good idea of what the next five minutes hold, but you're sure to be a lot fuzzier about what will happen 20 years from now. This uncertainty about the future, and the related risk, are normally built into bond prices.

As we discussed earlier, the longer the maturity of a bond, the more its price fluctuates with any movement in interest rates. For example, if yields on 30-year Treasuries are 7.5 percent, a 1 percentage point rise in interest rates to 8.5 percent might make a one-year bond's price fall by 5 percent, while a 30-year bond's price might plunge 30 percent. Conversely, a 1 percent drop in interest rates would translate into a 5 percent rise in a one-year bond's price but a 40 percent rise in the price of a 30-year issue. Keep this extra volatility in mind if you plan to buy a longer term bond. While you usually receive a higher yield, it comes at the price of much more price fluctuation over the life of the bond.

The *yield curve* is a convenient chart allowing you to compare the current yields of short-term, medium-term, and long-term bonds. Though there are yield curves for many different kinds of bonds, the curve you will see most often is for Treasury securities. The Treasury curve is printed daily in *The Wall Street Journal* and

Fig. ⑱ Treasury Yield Curve

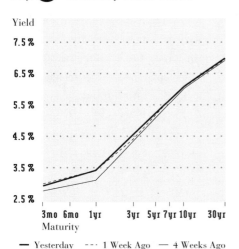

— Yesterday   --- 1 Week Ago   — 4 Weeks Ago

Source: Adapted and used by permission of *The Wall Street Journal*, ©1993 Dow Jones & Company, Inc. All Rights Reserved Worldwide

Fig. ⑲ Positive Yield Curve

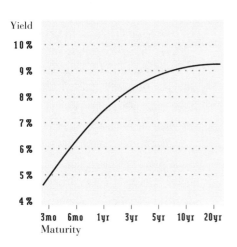

other newspapers and also appears in financial magazines. A typical yield curve looks like Figure 18.

Across the bottom of the chart are the various bond maturities, from the shortest maturity of three months to the longest maturity of 30 years. Down the side of the chart are the various yields on Treasury securities. This particular chart shows potential yields ranging from a high of 7.5 percent to a low 2.5 percent yield. The curve illustrates how much more interest a bond with a longer maturity earns. In this case, for instance, a 30-year bond pays nearly 7 percent, while a three-month bill pays only about 3.25 percent. The difference between the long and the short maturity – in this case, 4.25 percentage points – is the premium investors currently demand for committing their money for a long time. When long-term interest rates are much higher than short-term rates, as in this case, bond experts call the resulting curve a *steeply- sloped positive yield curve.*

At other times, the difference between short- and long-maturity bonds can be very slight, producing a yield curve that looks like Figure 19.

Here, there is virtually no difference between three-month Treasury bills and 20-year bonds; both yield about 7 percent. This is known as a *flat yield curve* (see Figure 20).

An *abnormal yield curve* occurs when short-term rates are actually higher than long-term rates, usually when the economy is about to head into a recession. In this case, yields on three-month bills are 9.2 percent, while yields on 20-year bonds are 5 percent. This is known as a *negative*, or an *inverted*, yield curve (see Figure 21). An inverted yield curve occurred briefly in the early 1980s, for instance, when the Federal Reserve pushed up interest rates

Fig. 20 Flat Yield Curve

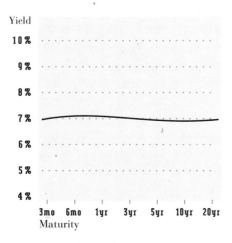

Fig. 21 Inverted Yield Curve

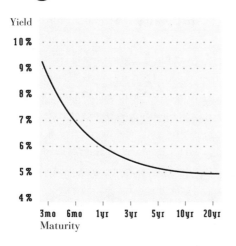

sharply to combat inflation, while long-term rates rose more gradually.

When choosing the maturity of a bond, you might look for the "sweet spot" on the yield curve. This is the maturity at which you receive the highest possible yield for the lowest possible risk. No definitive sweet spot exists; it varies according to the shape of the yield curve and your view of the direction of interest rates.

[Types of Bonds: Choosing the Best for You]

Now that you understand the basics of bonds, it is time to discuss the advantages and disadvantages of the many kinds of bonds that exist. Selecting the best bond for you depends on the size of your assets, your financial goals, your risk tolerance, your tax situation, and your knowledge level. The following sections touch on each kind of bond, starting with the most conservative (Treasuries) and ending with the most speculative (junk bonds).

Treasury Bonds

Bonds issued by the U.S. government are considered the safest around because Uncle Sam has a weapon to back these bonds that no other entity has: the printing press. If the government does not have enough funds to honor its debts, it can always print more money. When Congress raises the national debt ceiling every year or two, the government is, in effect, giving itself permission to borrow more money. This is known as the full faith and credit of the U.S. government, and it backs every Treasury security.

From a bond investor's point of view, *Treasury bonds* trade as though they are free from the risk of default. No one can even envision a default on Treasury bonds; the government must borrow money constantly in order to operate. It would be totally against the government's interest to default because the government would never again be able to sell bonds in the market, thus ensuring the government's instant collapse.

Because Treasuries are considered immune from default, they are the benchmark against which all other bonds are compared. Treasuries are to the bond world what diamonds are to the precious gem world: Nothing is more secure than a Treasury, and no stone is harder than a diamond. Whenever you investigate another bond's default risk, yield, after-tax return, and ease of trading, compare it to what a Treasury offers. Treasury notes work just like bonds except that notes are shorter maturities.

Treasury bonds are issued in minimum denominations of $1,000 and also in $5,000, $10,000, $100,000 and $1 million sizes. To invest in Treasury bonds, you put up your $1,000 (or more) and receive interest checks every six months.

Under a program called Treasury Direct, you can have your interest checks deposited electronically in any bank or financial institution you choose.

Treasury bills, discussed in more detail on p.13, mature in a year or less and come in minimum denominations of $10,000. To invest in Treasury bills, you pay less than the $10,000 face amount but receive $10,000 when the bill matures. So, for example, you might pay $9,500 for a three-month Treasury bill, and in three months, you get $10,000. The $500 in interest you received means the bill yielded 5.26 percent. To calculate your yield on a Treasury bill, divide the interest by the amount you invested.

$$\frac{\$500 \text{ Interest earned}}{\$9,500 \text{ Capital invested}} = 5.26\% \text{ Yield on Treasury bill}$$

If you buy Treasury securities directly from a Federal Reserve bank or branch or the Bureau of Public Debt (1300 C St., S.W., Washington, DC 20239), you do not have to pay any fees. The easiest way to buy directly is to put in a so-called noncompetitive bid at one of the Treasury's quarterly auctions, which usually occur in February, May, August, and November. Entering such a bid means you will accept whatever average rate emerges for the securities you want to buy. If you buy a Treasury security through a regular bank or brokerage firm, it will charge a modest fee of between $50 and $60.

Because literally trillions of dollars' worth of outstanding Treasury securities exist, the market for them is huge, and it is extremely easy to buy or sell them. But remember, just because Treasuries are free from default risk does not mean you can't lose money on them. If you buy when rates are low and sell after rates have risen, the value of your Treasury bond will fall. On the other hand, if you buy when rates are high and sell after rates have fallen, you can capture a capital gain, on which you must pay a capital gains tax.

Treasuries have another feature quite unique in the bond world. Almost all Treasury bonds are *noncallable*. That means the Treasury cannot redeem them before maturity, as many corporations and municipalities can do with their bonds. In some rare cases, Treasuries may be redeemed early, but for the most part, you are able to lock in the current rate on a Treasury for much longer than you are with any other bond. Just ask any of those happy investors who, in the early 1980s, bought 30-year Treasury bonds with 13 percent yields. Despite the decade-long plunge in rates that followed, they are still collecting their 13 percent interest every six months.

U.S. government bonds have another advantage that many people do not realize: All the interest you earn is exempt from state and local taxes. As part of the U.S. Constitution, a separation of federal and state powers was set up so that states cannot tax federal securities. In addition, the federal government cannot tax state and local securities. This is why, for residents of the issuing state, municipal bonds are exempt from federal taxes. By avoiding state and local taxes on Treasury securities, your effective after-tax yield is actually a bit higher than you might think, particularly if you live in a high-tax city or state. For example, say you own a Treasury bond worth $10,000 that is yielding 10 percent, or $1,000, a year. If your combined city and state tax rate is 10 percent, you have avoided paying the $100 in local taxes that would have been due if Treasury interest were not exempt. You still must pay federal income tax on your Treasury bond interest, of course.

Treasuries have all these wonderful features, but what is their disadvantage? In return for the safety, liquidity, and tax advantages, you receive a lower yield than is available from other bonds. How much lower depends on the current market conditions and the bonds to which you compare Treasuries. But for conservative income-oriented investors, there's no match for Treasuries.

U.S. Savings Bonds

Even though savings bonds are another form of Treasury security, they have several features that are worth discussing separately. Like other Treasuries, savings bonds have the backing of the full faith and credit of the U.S. government, and the interest they pay is free from state and local taxes. Unlike other Treasuries, though, savings bonds have the following features.

• *They are available in much smaller denominations.* You can buy a savings bond at any bank, or through your company by payroll deduction, for as little as $25 apiece. They also come in denominations of $50, $75, $100, $200, $500, $1,000, $5,000, and $10,000. The government limits you to investing a maximum of $15,000 a year in savings bonds.

• *Series EE savings bonds are issued at half their face value.* When you buy a $50 bond, for example, you pay $25 for it. They have no set maturity date and pay no current interest, but you can redeem them any time – from within six months of buying them to as long as 30 years later, according to a redemption schedule published by the Treasury Department. You owe federal tax on the interest earned only when you redeem the bonds.

• *You can swap noninterest-bearing Series EE bonds for a minimum of $500 worth of Series HH bonds, which pay cash interest at a 4 percent rate.* You must pay taxes on the cash interest for the tax year in which you receive the checks. But when you swap, you do not have to pay taxes on all the interest your EEs accumulated until you redeem the HHs. Series HH bonds mature in 10 years.

• *Yields on U.S. savings bonds are not fixed.* Instead, you receive a rate equal to 85 percent of the five-year Treasury rate over the time you own them. Therefore, you are protected if interest rates rise because the yield you earn will also rise.

• *The government guarantees a minimum yield if you hold the bonds for at least five years.* For several years, the minimum had been 6 percent, which meant you earned a higher yield on savings bonds than on equivalent five-year Treasury securities. In 1993, the government lowered the guaranteed minimum to 4 percent.

• *If your modified adjusted gross income is between $45,500 and $60,500 for individuals, or $68,250 and $98,250 for married couples filing jointly, at the time you redeem your savings bonds (this amount is adjusted slightly upward for inflation every year) the interest you earn from the bonds is either fully or partially tax exempt if you use it for college tuition for either yourself or your children.* Make sure to keep the savings bonds in your own name if you plan on using the proceeds for educational expenses.

As you can see, savings bonds have a lot going for them. If you sign up to receive them as part of a payroll savings plan, you receive an added benefit: You build capital automatically, which will come in handy if you need quick cash for an emergency or when you need capital to live on in retirement.

Government Agency Securities

One notch more risky than Treasuries and savings bonds are the securities issued by a plethora of federal government-backed agencies. Though they do not have the full faith and credit of the U.S. government behind them, you can be certain Congress would find a way to make sure these agencies don't default on their debt. Take the savings and loan crisis, for example. Congress appropriated a few hundred billion dollars to make sure depositors covered by the Federal Savings and Loan Insurance Corporation (FSLIC) would not lose their money. Though the specific laws backing each agency are different, the effect is the same: A default is almost unthinkable.

Because agency securities are not considered as completely risk-free as Treasury securities, they pay slightly higher yields. If a Treasury bond yields 8 percent, a federal agency security of the same maturity might pay from 8.25 percent to 9 percent, for instance. Like interest from Treasuries, interest from agency securities is usually taxable at the federal level but exempt from state and local taxes. As with any bond, you must pay a capital gains tax if you sell a federal agency bond for a profit. The two major exceptions to this rule are mortgage-backed securities of the Federal National Mortgage Association (Fannie Mae) and the Government National Mortgage Association (Ginnie Mae). (The next section discusses mortgage-backed securities in more detail.)

Unlike Treasuries, federal agency securities are not auctioned directly to the public; they are sold by a network of bond dealers and banks. Nonetheless, they are easy to buy through any brokerage firm. The dealer usually does not charge an explicit commission on agency securities (or on most other bonds), but he or she marks up the bonds and earns a profit on the spread between the price the dealer paid for them and the price at which he or she sells them. Depending on the agency, the bonds come in minimum denominations of $1,000 to $25,000.

The agencies that issue securities to the public are numerous and varied in their public purpose. The following is a list of the biggest issuers of government-backed paper, with their acronyms or nicknames, where applicable.

Asian Development Bank
College Construction Loan Insurance Corporation (Connie Lee)
Export-Import Bank of the United States
Farmers Home Administration (FmHA)
Federal Agricultural Mortgage Corporation (Farmer Mac)
Federal Farm Credit System
Federal Home Loan Bank System (FHLB)
Federal Home Loan Mortgage Corporation (Freddie Mac)
Federal Housing Administration (FHA)
Federal National Mortgage Association (Fannie Mae)
Government National Mortgage Association (Ginnie Mae)
International Bank for Reconstruction and Development (World Bank)
Resolution Funding Corporation (Refcorp)
Small Business Administration (SBA)
Student Loan Marketing Association (Sallie Mae)
Tennessee Valley Authority (TVA)
United States Postal Service

Some of these agencies are fully owned by the government; therefore, their securities are considered nearly as safe as Treasuries. Such agencies include the Export-Import Bank, the Farmers Home Administration, the FHA, Ginnie Mae, the TVA, and the Postal Service. Many of the agencies that are fully owned by the government issue securities through the Federal Financing Bank, established in 1974 as a central clearinghouse for federal agencies to issue debt.

Most of the other agencies listed were originally fully owned by the government but have since been transferred either to public ownership or to ownership by the organizations that benefit from the agency's services. For example, Fannie Mae, Freddie Mac and Sallie Mae are all publicly traded corporations, with their stocks trading on the NYSE. The FHLB is owned by its member banks.

Whether a federal agency bond is right for you depends on its current yield and whether you feel comfortable with the slightly greater risk involved in owning one. For most conservative income-oriented investors, it can be a fine choice.

Mortgage-Backed Securities

You may not realize it, but when you take out a mortgage from your local bank or savings and loan, your monthly mortgage payments are probably funneled by the bank or S&L through a federally designed system to investors who buy mortgage-backed securities. These securities, which go by the names of the agencies that guarantee timely payment of the securities' interest and principal, such as Ginnie Mae, Fannie Mae, and Freddie Mac, offer higher yields than Treasury bonds at slightly higher levels of risk.

A *mortgage-backed security* works as follows: Soon after a bank or savings and loan issues a mortgage to a homeowner, the loan is sold along with thousands of other loans to a federal agency, which repackages them in the form of a mortgage-backed security. The federal agency then guarantees it will pay investors interest and principal as they come due, even if a homeowner is late with his or her mortgage payments or defaults on the mortgage. The homeowner continues to make payments to the local bank, which collects a fee from the agency for providing this go-between service. Once the bank receives this money, it can make another mortgage loan and start the process again.

From the investor's point of view, a mortgage-backed security provides regular monthly interest as it is paid by homeowners. In addition, each month a certain amount of the mortgage principal is repaid, and that money is also passed through to the investor. The investor's brokerage statement will distinguish the two types of income he or she receives from the security each month.

The mortgage-backed securities market, which began in 1970 when Ginnie Mae introduced the concept, has mushroomed. Hundreds of billions of dollars' worth of outstanding mortgage-backed securities now exist, and billions of dollars' worth more are created every year. These securities are actively traded, and plenty of such bonds are always available from any major brokerage firm. However, several problems exist for small investors buying individual mortgage-backed securities. First, the minimum denomination is $25,000 though some older issues trading at lower prices may require less than that. Second, the timing of interest and principal payments is not totally predictable. This is the biggest difference between a mortgage-backed security and a Treasury bond, which pays interest every six months and is not callable for years.

The interest and principal repayment schedule is uncertain because the homeowners making the payments can be unpredictable. If mortgage rates fall enough to make it worthwhile, they will refinance their higher interest mortgages. On the other hand, if mortgage rates rise, homeowners will hold onto their mortgages for dear life. And if a homeowner sells the residence, he or she may have to pay off the mortgage and take out another loan for his or her new home. Because the mortgage-backed security is a conduit through which homeowner payments pass, all of this activity greatly affects the cash flow received by investors.

In certain situations, the investors in a mortgage-backed security lose whichever way interest rates go. For instance, say an investor buys a Ginnie Mae filled with 10 percent mortgages, and mortgage rates drop over the next few years to 7 percent. Many of the homeowners in that Ginnie Mae pool will refinance their mortgages to lock in 7 percent, causing the investor to receive a flood of principal at a time when interest rates have fallen and it is impossible to replicate that 10 percent yield. In another scenario, if interest rates soar from 10 percent to 13 percent, exactly the reverse would happen. Few, if any, homeowners would refinance their mortgages at higher rates, so the investor would receive only a small amount of principal. With rates at 13 percent, though, the investor would love to receive principal so he or she could reinvest it at the higher rates.

As the mortgage-backed securities market has matured over the last two decades, these problems have become well recognized. The mortgage-backed securities industry has reacted in two ways: by raising yields and by creating new forms of mortgage-backed paper. To compensate investors for the uncertainty about the pace of repayment, mortgage-backed securities now pay between 1 and 2 percentage points more than Treasury securities of similar maturities. So, if a 10-year Treasury is paying 8 percent, you might be able to earn as much as 10 percent from a Ginnie Mae or Fannie Mae.

As though regular mortgage-backed securities were not complicated enough, a newer and even more complex version called a *collateralized mortgage obligation* (CMO), or a *real estate mortgage investment conduit* (REMIC), has been invented to ease the prepayment worry. In theory, a CMO or REMIC works by slicing a mortgage-backed securities pool into *tranches* (the French word for slices). All prepayments from underlying mortgages are applied to the first tranche until it is paid off. Then prepayments are applied to the next tranche until it is redeemed, and so on, until all the tranches are eventually retired. The idea behind this slice-and-dice routine is that investors will be able to choose a tranche that most closely meets their maturity needs and will have a better chance that the security will last that long. Yet because tranches still do not guarantee prepayment schedules, investors receive a yield that is 1 to 3 percentage points higher than they would earn on similar maturity Treasuries.

Even though all this sounds extremely complicated, billions of dollars flow into mortgage-backed securities, CMOs, and REMICs these days, as people search out higher yields than are available from bank CDs and money-market funds. Realizing this, brokers market CMOs aggressively. Mortgage-backed securities may be right for you, as long as you understand what you are getting into.

In addition to mortgage-backed securities, there exist several new classes of securities backed by other types of loans. These work exactly like mortgage-backed paper. The latest forms of asset-backed securities include pools of credit card loans, car loans, mobile home loans, and college loans. If you consider buying into one of these innovative loan pools, apply the same criteria you used with mortgage-backed securities.

Municipal Bonds

Though riskier than Treasury or agency securities, *municipal bonds* (munis) are extremely popular. These bonds, issued by states, cities, counties, towns, villages, and taxing authorities of many types, have one feature that separates them from all other securities: The interest they pay is totally free from federal taxes. In most cases, bondholders who are also residents of the states issuing the bonds do not have to pay state or local taxes on the interest either. (For a list of which states tax bonds and which do not, see the end of this section.) Bonds not taxable by the resident state are known as *double-tax-free bonds*, and those also not taxable by a locality are called *triple-tax-free issues.* The exemption from federal taxation is based on the 1895 Supreme Court case of *Pollock vs. Farmers' Loan and Trust Company*, which applied the constitutional doctrine of "intergovernmental tax immunity." The High Court ruled that this doctrine means that states are immune from federal interference with their ability to borrow money.

The fact that the interest from municipal bonds is federally tax free allows issuers to float bonds with yields lower than taxable government and corporate bond issuers must pay. Investors are satisfied to earn 6 percent tax free, compared with 8 percent on a Treasury, on which federal taxes are due. The higher an investor's federal, state, and local tax bracket, the more attractive munis become because they permit the investor to escape more taxes. At the same time, the lower yields that municipalities pay make it affordable for them to build roads, schools, sewer systems, hospitals, and other public facilities.

The market for municipal bonds is huge: Several hundred billion dollars' worth of bonds are outstanding, and billions of dollars' worth of new bonds are issued every year. While there exist millions of bonds and thousands of issuers, no centralized marketplace trades munis as it does stocks. Instead, municipal bonds are bought and sold by the many brokerage firms and banks that specialize in them. These dealers communicate with each other through a telephone and computer network. To buy municipal bonds, you must go through a broker or bank that can plug into this complex system of competing dealers. As with other bonds, brokers usually do not charge a separate commission to buy or sell your municipal issue. Instead, they make their money by marking up the bond from their cost by about 2 percent.

Municipal bonds are usually issued in minimum denominations of $5,000, though some are issued in lots as small as $1,000. Brokers usually require a minimum order of $5,000, but they prefer dealing in blocks of five bonds, or $25,000. Small orders invariably are hit with markups as high as 5 percent. Depending on the dollar volume of the bonds when they are issued, trading can be very active or almost nonexistent. Many municipalities have issued only a few bonds during their history, so the bonds are hard to buy or sell. If you plan to buy a bond and hold it until maturity, the fact that little trading activity occurs should be of little concern to you. When shopping for a municipal bond, ask how many years of protection against early redemption you will receive. Many municipal bond investors have been shocked in recent years when they received their principal back much sooner than they expected it.

Two main types of municipal bonds exist: *general obligation* and *revenue* bonds. General obligation bonds (GOs) are issued by a state or local entity and are backed by the taxing power of that state, city, or town. In general, the proceeds from these issues are used to finance general capital expenditures, as well as ongoing municipal operations. Revenue bonds, on the other hand, finance specific revenue-producing projects, such as toll roads, bridges, tunnels, sewer systems, or airports. The interest and principal paid by the bonds come from the economic activity generated by the bonds. For instance, a revenue bond might be floated to finance a new highway. The proceeds of the issue will be spent to build the road, and tolls collected on the road for the next several years will pay the interest and principal on the bonds. You can buy many other forms of revenue bonds, some riskier than others. For example, so-called private purpose bonds can be issued on behalf of hospitals, universities, or other nonprofit organizations. Industrial revenue bonds are sponsored by municipalities to finance construction of factories or industrial parks that will bring jobs into a district.

Aside from different kinds of general obligation and revenue bonds, some municipal issues can be taxable under certain circumstances. For example, some bonds are issued to be subject to federal income tax but exempt from state and local taxes to in-state residents who buy them. Other bonds, known as *alternative minimum tax* (AMT) bonds, can be taxed if the holder falls into the alternative minimum tax trap, which is designed to keep wealthy people from avoiding federal taxes altogether. If the holder will not be hit by the AMT, these bonds, which pay a slightly higher yield than regular munis, would provide totally tax-free income.

Debates rage among bond analysts over whether general obligation or revenue bonds are safer for investors. To some extent, the safety of the bond depends on the financial situation of the issuing entity and the revenue potential of the project the issue funds. Though defaults by states and cities are exceedingly rare, they can happen if political gridlock occurs in a state or city where expenses are soaring, revenues are falling, and residents are moving out. Revenue projects normally are a safe bet as well, but they can be disrupted if an economic contraction (the area's economy takes a downturn) in the area of the project causes revenues to come in under projections. The best way to judge the safety of any particular issue is to look at the bond's safety rating by Standard & Poor's, Moody's, or Fitch.

If you would rather not worry at all about safety, a conservative alternative called *municipal bond insurance* is becoming more widely available on a broad range of municipal bonds. You cannot buy insurance on your bonds individually, but you can purchase bonds that already have insurance attached to them. The municipal bond insurers, such as the Municipal Bond Investors Assurance Corporation (MBIA), the American Municipal Bond Assurance Corporation (AMBAC), and several others guarantee that you will receive timely payments of interest and principal for the life of the bond if the issuer defaults. Insured bonds usually trade as though they have an AAA rating because no risk of default exists. However, the cost of the insurance is passed on to the investor; insured bonds usually yield a little less than similar noninsured bonds.

Determining your taxable equivalent yield.
To calculate whether a municipal bond makes sense for you, compare its yield with taxable alternatives to see which bond leaves you the most money after taxes. The following exercise helps you determine the taxable equivalent yield of your muni.

First, deduct your federal tax bracket from 100. (This example uses a 31 percent tax bracket.) The result is known as the reciprocal of your tax bracket.

$$100 - 31 \text{ Tax bracket} = 69 \text{ Reciprocal of tax bracket}$$

Divide the tax-free yield on the municipal bond you are considering by the reciprocal of your tax bracket. (In this case, assume the bond pays a 7 percent tax-free yield.)

$$\frac{7\% \text{ Municipal bond yield}}{69 \text{ Reciprocal of tax bracket}} = 10.14\% \text{ Taxable equivalent yield}$$

The above calculation means you would have to buy a taxable bond paying 10.14 percent to end up with the same dollar amount after taxes that the 7 percent muni will pay. To earn that high a yield, you would normally have to take on far more risk than a municipal bond entails.

To make munis look even more attractive, go through the same exercise adding in your state and local tax brackets. For example, if your combined federal, state, and local tax brackets total 40 percent, the taxable equivalent yield of a 7 percent muni would be an astounding 11.6 percent! You can see why munis are so popular.

The following table will give you a few taxable equivalent yields for various tax-free muni yields. As you can see, the higher the tax bracket, the more you would have to earn in a taxable bond to end up with the same after-tax return.

Federal Tax Bracket	*Tax - Exempt Yield*				
	4%	*5%*	*6%*	*7%*	*8%*
15%	4.71%	5.88%	7.05%	8.23%	9.41%
28	5.56	6.94	8.33	9.72	11.11
31	5.80	7.25	8.70	10.14	11.59
36	6.25	7.81	9.37	10.93	12.50
39.6	6.62	8.27	9.93	11.58	13.24

Which states tax which bonds.

In almost every state, interest from bonds issued by that state is tax free to state residents. The only exceptions are Illinois, Iowa, Kansas, Oklahoma, and Wisconsin. For residents of those states, interest from some, but not all, in-state bonds is tax exempt.

The following states never impose state taxes on interest earned by residents who buy bonds issued by other states: Alaska, the District of Columbia, Indiana, Nevada, South Dakota, Texas, Utah, Washington, and Wyoming.

The following states do impose state taxes on interest earned by residents who buy bonds issued by other states:

Alabama	Hawaii	Massachusetts	New Mexico	South Carolina
Arizona	Idaho	Michigan	New York	Tennessee
Arkansas	Illinois	Minnesota	North Carolina	Vermont
California	Iowa	Mississippi	North Dakota	Virginia
Colorado	Kansas	Missouri	Ohio	West Virginia
Connecticut	Kentucky	Montana	Oklahoma	Wisconsin
Delaware	Louisiana	Nebraska	Oregon	
Florida	Maine	New Hampshire	Pennsylvania	
Georgia	Maryland	New Jersey	Rhode Island	

Keep these taxation rules in mind when you are deciding whether it makes more sense to buy an in-state bond or an out-of-state bond. Your return will depend on whether the out-of-state bond is taxable and on your state tax rates.

Clearly, if you are in a high enough tax bracket, it could be quite worthwhile to investigate municipal bonds. They are not only safe; their after-tax yields can often beat any other taxable alternative.

Corporate Bonds

The next rung down the ladder of bond risk are bonds issued by corporations. While the U.S. government and its agencies, states, and municipalities are not going to disappear, corporations may not be around forever. Thousands of companies go bankrupt each year. Firms thrive or crash based on their success in the marketplace, and that is never ensured. Because corporations, no matter how solid financially, are thus perceived as vulnerable to changes in the business environment, the bonds they issue are considered riskier than government issues and therefore always pay a higher yield than government issues of the same maturity.

Still, only a tiny percentage of corporate bonds – typically less than 1 percent – ever default. Thousands of perfectly solid issues are outstanding, and many more come to market every year. Even in the worst-case scenario of a company going bankrupt, bondholders' claims are settled before stockholders receive any compensation.

As an individual investor, you have many opportunities to increase your income by holding corporate bonds. Most bonds pay interest semiannually and use the electronic book-entry system, so interest payments can be sent automatically to your brokerage account. Depending on the financial creditworthiness of the issuing company, a corporate bond can yield from 2 to 6 percentage points more than Treasuries of the same maturity.

As with all bonds, you can profit by buying them when interest rates are high and selling them after rates have fallen and bond prices have climbed. Corporate bond prices react to general fluctuations in interest rates, as well as the financial fortunes (or misfortunes) of the issuing companies. For example, a bond's price will rise if the company's finances improve because investors anticipate that the bond's safety rating from agencies like Standard & Poor's might be upgraded. On the other hand, a series of financial setbacks will cause the bond's price to sink, as investors fear a rating downgrade. If the situation deteriorates enough, the bond's price might plummet to very low levels because investors think the firm might declare bankruptcy and default on its bond payments.

Corporate bonds typically are issued in denominations of $1,000 and quoted in units of $100, like Treasury bonds. Most bond dealers don't like trading in lots of fewer than five bonds, or less than $5,000. For smaller lots, brokers' markups can be quite high. In some cases, brokers will charge a minimum per-bond commission of as much as $20.

Many of the thousands of outstanding corporate bonds trade quite actively and are therefore easy to buy and sell. Some smaller issues may not trade as frequently, which means there will be a wider spread between the buying price and the selling price.

As with municipal bonds, you must research your protection against premature calls carefully. Many corporate bonds offer ten years guaranteed against early redemption though call protection varies widely. Among the most frustrating experiences for investors is to have a high-yield corporate bond plucked from their grasp after interest rates have fallen sharply. Corporate treasurers will always do whatever is in the best interest of their stockholders – which is to refinance high-yield debt at the first possible moment.

Most corporate bonds are unsecured, meaning they are backed only by the companies' general ability to repay them out of cash flow and profits. Such unsecured bonds are generally called *debentures*. Other corporate bonds are secured by a particular asset, which becomes the property of bondholders if a company defaults. Examples of secured corporate bonds include mortgage bonds, backed by real estate, and equipment trust certificates, backed by equipment such as airplanes or railroad cars.

While most corporate bonds are fairly conservative, junk bonds allow riskier investment. (An upcoming section describes junk bonds in more detail.)

Foreign Bonds

You need not restrict your search for solid, income-producing bonds to U.S. securities. There's a big world beyond our shores, and it is filled with opportunities in highly rated, high-yielding bonds issued by foreign governments and foreign-based corporations.

Foreign government bonds, like U.S. Treasuries, are backed by the full faith and credit of the issuing countries. While that sounds comforting, the guarantee has more weight coming from an industrialized country like Germany or France than from a developing country like Kenya or Costa Rica. In some places where political turbulence seems to be a local tradition, like Argentina or Haiti, protecting the interests of bondholders is not usually high on the latest ruler's priority list. Because most investors do not want to have to worry about receiving their interest and principal, the foreign government bonds that trade most actively in the United States are issued by industrialized countries.

Most U.S. brokers can sell foreign government bonds, though the easiest ones to trade are so-called *Yankee bonds*, which are issued in the United States by foreign governments and are denominated in dollars. It is probably not worth the hassle of buying a bond denominated in a foreign currency and having to convert interest payments in francs, pounds, or deutsche marks into dollars. Most foreign bonds, even Yankee bonds, come in minimum denominations much higher than the denominations of domestic issues. Depending on the country, you might have to invest at least $25,000 to buy one German or French bond, for instance.

Foreign corporate bonds have drawbacks similar to foreign government bonds. The bonds that are most actively traded are those issued by large, well-known, foreign-based corporations like Sony in Japan, Barclays Bank in the United Kingdom, Michelin in France, or Siemens in Germany. In many cases, you can find a Yankee bond that pays interest in U.S. dollars. Minimum investments still tend to be higher than they are for domestic bonds, often running in the $25,000 range.

Foreign bonds might make sense for you for two reasons. First, the yields on foreign bonds can be significantly higher than those on similar domestic issues. In the mid-1990s, for example, yields on most European bonds were 4 to 5 percentage points higher than on U.S. bonds. This was because the German central bank was determined to battle the inflationary impact of the reconstruction of Eastern Germany by keeping interest rates high. Because most European currencies were linked to the German mark, European central banks had to keep their rates high as well. The result was billions of dollars of U.S. money rushing into the European bond market to capture those high yields.

The other reason foreign bonds can be profitable is that their value to U.S. investors can rise if the U.S. dollar falls against the foreign currencies. So, in the best of all worlds, your foreign bond can give you not only a high yield but capital gains as well.

When you buy a foreign bond, you are, in effect, converting your dollars into the bond's foreign currency. If that currency appreciates against the dollar, you will have earned a profit when you convert the bond back into dollars. To take a highly exaggerated example, say you buy a $1,000 bond denominated in British pounds when you get two pounds for one U.S. dollar. If, over the next few years, the British pound appreciates so you get one pound for each dollar, you will double your money from $1,000 to $2,000. The following breaks down this exaggerated example to determine your potential gain. (This example is for illustration only; the dollar-pound relationship does not fluctuate this widely.) When buying the bond:

$1,000 = 2,000 pounds, with an exchange rate of one dollar for two pounds

When selling the bond:

2,000 pounds = $2,000, with an exchange rate of one dollar for one pound

Profit: $1,000 or 100%.

Of course, if the value of the dollar appreciates against the foreign currency, you will lose money when you translate the bond back into dollars. Therefore, when you consider buying a foreign bond, evaluate whether the dollar seems to be getting stronger or weaker. It's best to wait until you think the dollar is getting weaker.

Despite the potential high yields and profits from foreign bonds, most individuals play this market by buying mutual funds that specialize in foreign bonds. Funds allow investors to avoid the complexities and high cost of buying individual foreign bonds, yet they offer high yields and the play on the U.S. dollar. (For more on foreign bond funds, see p.98.)

Zero-Coupon Bonds

Zero-coupon bonds – called zeros for short – can, paradoxically, be the safest of all investments or the riskiest. It all depends on how you use them.

A zero-coupon bond gets its name from the fact that the bond is issued with a 0 percent coupon rate. Because people buy bonds to collect interest at the coupon rate, who would ever be interested in a bond that pays no interest? Plenty of people, and here's why:

Instead of making regular interest payments, a zero is issued at a deep discount from its face value of 100, or $5,000. The return on a zero comes from the gradual increase in the bond's price from the discount to face value, which it reaches at maturity.

This slow but steady rise in value yields three benefits.

1. You know exactly how much money you will receive when the bond matures.

2. You know exactly when you will receive that money.

3. You do not have to worry about reinvesting the small amounts of interest regular full-coupon bonds pay.

Very few investments can guarantee you will receive a specific dollar amount years from now. Because zeros have a specific schedule of appreciation, you can use a zero as an integral part of a financial plan to fund specific expenses years in advance. For example, if you are the parent of a newborn, you know to the month when his or her first college tuition payment will be due. Therefore, you can buy a zero maturing in 18 years. Or, if you are a 40-year-old who plans to retire at age 65, you can buy a 25-year zero that will mature on the day your company gives you the gold watch.

When you contact a broker about buying a zero, he or she will usually quote the current price of a bond that will mature at a face value of $1,000 a number of years in the future (one advantage is that you can buy almost any amount, not a minimum of $5,000), and he or she will tell you what yield you are locking in at that price. The broker's quote will include the markup, so you do not have to figure in an additional commission. Markups can vary widely from broker to broker, so it is important that you shop around. Get at least three quotes, asking for:

• the amount of money you must invest now, including all fees and commissions;
• the amount of money you will receive when the zero matures on the date you choose; and
• the yield to maturity you will be locking in for the years you hold the zero.

Once you have the data for various zeros, choose the bond selling for the lowest price and boasting the highest yield to maturity for the date you want.

For example, if you want to have a lump sum of $10,000 available to you at various times in the future, the following is a table typical of one a broker might give you. It outlines your bond options and lays out the prices and yields you might achieve.

Notice that the longer in the future you want your money back, the fewer dollars you must pay now because you are allowing more time for the zero to compound.

The other attraction of a zero is that your interest is reinvested automatically at the zero's yield. This can be a particularly significant advantage if you lock in a high interest rate. With a regular interest-paying bond, you receive interest checks every six months, which can be helpful if you need the money for living expenses. But if you would rather reinvest the interest to make your capital grow, prevailing interest rates constantly rise and fall, making it impossible to lock in a constant rate of reinvestment. Also, the dollar amount of your interest payment may be so small that you would not be able to afford the minimum needed to buy another bond.

	Current Price	Cost in Dollars	Yield
5-year zero	71.80	$7,180	6.05%
10-year zero	48.12	4,812	7.05
15-year zero	31.61	3,161	7.54
20-year zero	20.86	2,086	7.77
25-year zero	14.28	1,428	7.76

Many issuers of zero-coupon bonds exist, but most investors buy zeros based on Treasury bonds. These zeros are commonly known as *STRIPS*, which stands for *separate trading of registered interest and principal of securities.* Like any other Treasury, they are backed by the full faith and credit of the U.S. government and are noncallable. Some brokerage firms have launched their own versions of STRIPS, with names like Salomon Brothers' *CATS (cer-*

tificates of accrual on Treasury securities) and Merrill Lynch's *TIGRs (Treasury investment growth receipts)*. In a sense, U.S. savings bonds are also zeros; they work exactly the same way but are issued in much smaller denominations. Also, several large corporations issue zero-coupon bonds that allow you to lock in higher yields than do government issues. For the most part, though, it is best to invest in STRIPS because you do not want to wait 20 years with no payoff, only to discover that the issuing corporation went bankrupt recently.

If you want a diversified portfolio of zeros, you can buy shares in a zero-coupon bond mutual fund for a minimum of $1,000. The two largest fund companies offering zero-coupon funds are the Benham Group (1665 Charleston Rd., Mountain View, CA 94043; 800-472-3389) and Scudder (175 Federal St., Boston, MA 02110; 800-225-2470). Benham offers no-load funds called target trusts that are set to mature every five years (such as 1995, 2000, 2005, 2010, 2015 and 2020). You pay annual expenses of .70 percent of your assets. Scudder offers one target trust; annual expenses are capped at 1 percent. You can avoid these expenses by buying STRIPS directly. But the fund does offer you a more diversified portfolio, and it is easy to buy and sell without having to pay the large spread some brokers charge.

Taxable zero-coupon bonds have one major pitfall. The Internal Revenue Service (IRS) has ruled that the scheduled yearly growth in the value of a zero-coupon bond (the IRS calls it the bond's accretion) must be considered interest income in the year it is earned, even though you do not receive any cash interest payments. The IRS publishes an accretion table, telling you how much "imputed" interest you must report each year. This rule can take much of the zip out of zeros because every year, you must pay taxes on interest without having received the interest to pay the taxes.

You have two ways to get around this dilemma: buying zeros only in tax-sheltered accounts or buying tax-free municipal zero-coupon bonds. If you buy a zero through an individual retirement account (IRA), a Keogh account, an annuity, a salary reduction plan, or some other vehicle that allows you to defer tax liability until you withdraw money from the account, the IRS accretion rules do not affect you. The zero compounds year after year, untouched by taxes. You pay taxes on the increased value only when you withdraw the money, usually at retirement.

Because you never owe taxes on the interest paid by municipal bonds, the same holds true for muni zeros. You can therefore buy muni zeros in your regular account and watch them compound tax free until they mature. The fact that muni zeros offer such superb benefits makes them extremely popular, which often means they sell out soon after they are issued. Therefore, if you think a muni zero is right for you, contact your broker before a new bond is issued so he or she can prepare to grab a few bonds while they last. When shopping for muni zeros, look carefully at the call provisions of the issues because many allow issuers to redeem them before their scheduled maturity, which could defeat your whole purpose in buying them. Figure 22 is an illustration of how a municipal zero would grow from $5,000 when you bought it to $20,000 in 20 years.

The risky side of zeros.

So far, we have described zeros as the safest and surest way to fund a distant financial goal, despite one major pitfall. However, another far more volatile side to zeros exists if you use zeros to earn capital gains.

Because zeros lock in a fixed reinvestment rate of interest for a long time, their prices react to fluctuations in interest rates far more than does any other type of bond. For every one-point drop in interest rates over a year, for example, a normal 30-year coupon bond paying 8 percent would produce a total return (price change plus income) of 20 percent, while a 30-year zero with an 8 percent reinvestment rate would soar by 42 percent. Conversely, if interest rates rose by 1 percentage point over a year, the full-coupon bond would suffer a negative total return of 3 percent, while the zero would plunge by 19 percent. The fact that the zero compounds its yield automatically for many years magnifies the impact of interest rate changes.

Fig. 22 Growth of 20-Year Municipal Zero-Coupon Bond

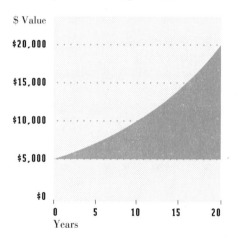

$ Value

$20,000

$15,000

$10,000

$5,000

$0

0   5   10   15   20
Years

Source: Adapted and used by permission of Public Securities Association

Figure 23 shows how the total return of a 30-year zero-coupon Treasury bond with an 8 percent reinvestment rate is affected by interest rate changes of 1 percentage point upward and downward over a year, compared to the effect on a 30-year full-coupon bond paying 8 percent.

Notice that the effect of a 1-percentage-point change is not symmetrical. A one-point drop yields a 43 percent gain on a zero, while a one-point rise yields an 18 percent loss.

Fig. **23** Zeros Versus Full-Coupon Bonds

	Percentage Point Change in a Year								
	+4	+3	+2	+1	Unchanged	-1	-2	-3	-4
30-year zero	−64%	−53%	−38%	−18%	+8%	+43%	+89%	+139%	+220%
30-year full-coupon	−24	−18	−11	−2	+8	+20	+35	+54	+76

Source: Courtesy of Ryan Labs, Inc., a bond research firm in New York, NY.

The effect of interest rate changes on zeros is lessened if the zeros are of a shorter maturity. This is obvious in Figure 24, which illustrates the effect of interest rate changes of 1 percentage point upward and downward on 5-, 10-, 20- and 30-year zeros. (The table assumes 30-year Treasury rates are at 8 percent.)

Fig. **24** 5-, 10-, 20-, and 30-Year Zeros Responding to Rate Changes

	Percentage Point Change in a Year								
	+4	+3	+2	+1	Unchanged	-1	-2	-3	-4
30-year zero	-64%	-53%	-38%	-18%	+8%	+43%	+89%	+139%	+220%
20-year zero	-47	-37	-25	-10	+8	+30	+56	+88	+117
10-year zero	-23	-16	-9	0	+8	+18	+29	+40	+53
5-year zero	-7	-4	0	+4	+8	+12	+17	+21	+26

Source: Courtesy of Ryan Labs, Inc., a bond research firm in New York, NY.

Notice that if interest rates drop by 4 percentage points, the 30-year zero would soar 220 percent, while the five-year zero would rise only 26 percent. On the other extreme, if rates shoot up by 4 percentage points, the 30-year bond would plummet 64 percent, while the five-year zero would fall only 7 percent. This dramatically illustrates that the longer the maturity of the zero, the more volatile its price will be.

As a result of zeros' volatility, they are the favorite weapon for speculators who want to bet that interest rates will fall. This is a game for serious investors, however, because if interest rates rise instead of fall, they can lose big. For most investors, though, zeros are far from a speculative investment.

Convertible Bonds

Convertible bonds are hybrids – one part bond and the other part stock. In their role as bonds, they offer regular fixed income though usually at a yield lower than straight bonds of the same issuer. In their role as stocks, convertibles offer significant appreciation potential and a way to benefit from the issuing companies' financial success. However, owners of convertibles will not benefit as much as common stockholders if the companies' fortunes soar. To some investors, convertibles offer the best of both worlds – high income and appreciation potential. To others, convertibles offer the worst of both worlds – lower income than bonds yield and less appreciation potential than common stock offers. Whichever way you view them, convertibles can make a solid contribution to your investment portfolio.

Convertibles come in two forms: *preferred stock* and *debentures*, which are unsecured bonds. Both pay a fixed rate of interest and are convertible into common stock of the issuer when the common stock reaches a certain price, known as the *conversion price*. That conversion price is always set at a level higher than the common stock's price at the time the convertible is first issued. It can be as low as 15 percent above the common price or as high as 50 percent above. When the underlying stock hits the conversion price, the convertible bond can be changed into a specified number of shares at what is called the *conversion ratio*. For example, ABC Corporation may issue a convertible that allows its holders to convert each bond into 50 shares of ABC common when ABC hits $100 a share.

Convertible bond prices are influenced by several factors. Because they are bonds, they are affected by the general ups and downs of interest rates. Also, the market evaluates convertibles as straight fixed-income securities. This gives them their investment value. The market also evaluates convertibles based on their underlying common stock. This gives them their conversion value. When the market takes a dim view of an underlying company, the convertible's investment value is more important than it would be otherwise. If the underlying company is a hot growth stock, however, the convertible will trade more on its conversion value because investors expect the common stock price to rise, and the convertible will eventually be changed into common shares.

You can judge what kind of growth potential the market expects of a convertible by looking at what is known as the *premium over conversion value*. As the underlying common stock rises in value, the convertible is viewed increasingly as a common stock. At a certain point, usually when the dividend on the underlying common stock is more valuable than the interest return from the convertible, it makes sense to convert into common shares. The price of the common shares will rise beyond the convertible price when this happens, signaling that it is time to convert.

The higher the conversion premium, the riskier the bond, however, because the premium can shrink quickly if the hot growth company stumbles. Any premium of more than 20 percent to 25 percent should be seen as a warning sign of increased risk. One way to protect yourself from paying too high a premium is to determine how long it will take to earn back that premium. The following example – in which the conversion premium is 20 percent, the underlying common stock yields 2 percent, and the convertible yields 7 percent – shows you how to do this.

First, subtract the common stock yield from the convertible yield.

Convertible yield	7%
Common stock yield	− 2%
Yield difference	5%

Then divide the premium by the yield difference.

$$20\% \div 5\% = 4 \text{ Years}$$

The answer indicates how long it would take to recover your conversion premium if all else stayed the same. In this case, it would take four years.

Convertible prices tend to fall less than stock prices when the stock market declines because convertibles offer a higher level of income than most stocks, which tends to cushion the convertibles' descent. On the other hand, when the stock market surges, convertibles tend to rise less than stocks.

Convertible bonds are usually denominated in minimums of $1,000, though most brokers like to trade at least ten bonds, or $10,000 worth, at a time. Smaller trades will subject you to larger dealer markups. Depending on the size of the convertible issue, the stature of the issuer and the credit rating of the bond from the ratings agencies, trading may be very active or inactive. As with other bonds, you must determine how much call protection the convertible offers. You don't want the bond redeemed quickly if interest rates fall and the issuer decides to refinance at a lower rate.

Convertibles offer no special tax breaks. All interest paid is fully taxable at the federal, state, and local levels. Although no taxes are due when you convert from a bond to common stock, you must pay all the normal taxes on the stock dividends. As with any other security, you must pay capital gains taxes if you sell a convertible for a profit.

Before you buy any convertible, decide whether you want to own the issuer's common stock. If you think the underlying company has a bright future, the convertible can be an excellent choice to improve your current income and profit from the firm's success. However, if you are considering the convertible only for the income, and you would not want to be caught holding the underlying stock, move on to another option. Despite all the bells and whistles of convertibles, they are ultimately just another way to invest in a company's prospects.

If you want the benefits of convertibles without the complications discussed here, you can invest in a convertible bond mutual fund. It offers a high yield and appreciation potential, and the fund manager is an expert in picking through the somewhat bewildering world of convertibles.

For those seeking more information about convertibles, many brokerage firms publish research reports on widely traded issues. The two best newsletters that track the field are the *Value Line Convertibles* (711 Third Ave., New York, NY 10017; 800-634-3583) and the *RHM Convertible Survey* (172 Forest Ave., Glen Cove, NY 11542; 516-759-2904).

Junk Bonds

The riskiest type of bond is known in the brokerage industry as *high-yield bonds*, but colloquially they are known as *junk bonds*. These bonds barely existed before the 1980s takeover, leveraged buyout, and junk bond boom made them famous – or infamous, depending on your experience with them.

Junk bonds are issued by corporations that have less than an investment-grade rating. That means Standard & Poor's and Fitch rate them below BBB, and Moody's rates them below Baa. Companies earn such low ratings for two reasons: They are either on their way up or on their way down, financially speaking. The up-and-comers are companies that do not have the long track record of sales and earnings that the ratings agencies require to merit an investment-grade rating. Just because they do not have a top rating, however, does not make them bad companies; it just means they need more seasoning before their rating rises from the B into the A category.

The companies on their way down, often called fallen angels, are a different story. These corporations attained an investment-grade rating in years past by diligently increasing sales and profits. But some event or series of events changed all that, causing the ratings agencies to downgrade the firms' bonds. Possible events include a takeover financed with millions of dollars in new debt, a failed market strategy that saddles a firm with operating losses instead of profits, or a general downturn in the economy that undermines a firm's profitability so severely that the ratings agencies doubt its ability to pay interest on its outstanding bonds.

While a low safety rating might be bad news for a company, it is good news for investors because it means that the firm's bonds will pay a substantially higher yield than will securities issued by blue chip corporations. How much more depends on which issuers you compare, but decent-quality junk bonds often yield between 2 and 5 percentage points more than investment-grade issues. That can translate into yields of 9 percent to 15 percent. Lower-quality junk issues can pay up to 20 percent.

Think you've found your dream investment? Well, hold onto your money because those higher yields obviously come with higher risks. The chief risks follow.

• *The company can default.* The higher the yield, in fact, the more likely it is that the bond's interest rate will drop suddenly one day, from high double digits to zero as the high cost of servicing the debt becomes too much for the company to handle. When a company seeks protection from creditors in bankruptcy, interest payments to bondholders often cease. Default rates on junk bonds vary and, to a large degree, depend on the overall health of the economy. A vibrant economy will allow companies to earn the profits they need to meet their interest costs, meaning only 1 percent or 2 percent of all junk bonds might default in a year. But in a recession, junk bond default rates can soar to 8 percent or 10 percent if reduced sales and profits make it impossible to pay bond interest.

• *The company's bonds can be downgraded further.* Though not as serious as outright default, a junk bond with a BB rating can be downgraded to a B or even into the Cs, which would pummel the bond's price.

• *Interest rates can rise.* While that hurts the value of all bonds, it can be particularly harmful to companies already in a weakened financial condition.

• *The stock market can fall.* Because a junk bond's price is tied closely to the fate of the underlying company, a general drop in stock prices can spill over to the company's stock price, which will affect its bond price negatively.

• *There can be an imbalance of supply and demand.* In the 1980s, when billions of dollars' worth of new junk bonds were brought to market every year, the supply eventually outran the demand, causing bond prices to decline sharply. In addition, because of junk bond-related scandals and losses suffered by junk bond holders, Congress forced savings and loans to sell their junk bonds. Insurance companies were later ordered to liquidate their portfolios for the same reasons. And many other large institutions, such as pension funds, were also banned from buying junk bonds. All of this reduced demand for junk bonds even further. The main buyers of junk bonds now are individuals and mutual funds that raise money from individuals.

• *The liquidity of junk bond trading can dry up.* If bad news hits the market, such as an unexpected default, it can become very difficult to buy or sell bonds at a reasonable price. Dealers will execute trades only at enormous spreads that make it unattractive for investors to complete transactions.

• *Junk bonds can be called.* Companies do not voluntarily pay double-digit yields on their bonds; they are forced to do so. If their financial fortunes improve, or if interest rates fall, they will refinance those high-yielding bonds with lower-yielding bonds at the first possible opportunity.

Despite the risks, junk bonds can provide very high returns if they are chosen well. In selecting a high-yield bond, look for a company with improving finances rather than worsening finances that you hope will turn around some day.

Most junk bonds come in minimum denominations of $1,000, but if they are depressed, they may sell for far less than that. Brokers normally like to sell bonds in lots of at least five, or $5,000. They will charge a wide spread or a steep commission on smaller orders.

The interest you receive from a junk bond is fully taxable at the federal, state, and local levels. If you sell the bond for a gain, you must pay capital gains tax. If the company defaults on its bonds and ultimately liquidates, you can use the bond certificates to wallpaper your living room (unless you would rather not be reminded of your investment). You can also write off your losses against other capital gains and $3,000 of ordinary income.

If you feel skittish about buying individual junk bonds (and you should), a safer alternative is to buy a mutual fund that purchases a widely diversified portfolio of the toxic issues. That way, you have a professional manager picking through the junk for you.

Whether you invest in junk bonds depends on your ability to tolerate high risk in return for high yields and some potentially large capital gains. However, don't put too much of your money into junk bonds. The risk is just not worth the angst.

[Bond Mutual Funds]

If the process of choosing individual bonds seems too complicated, bond mutual funds might be right for you.

Mutual funds offer several advantages to bond investors. For the most part, the bond market is designed for large institutional players that buy blocks of bonds, millions of dollars at a time, rather than small investors who buy a few thousand dollars' worth of securities. Bonds can be difficult to trade in small lots, so funds offer much better liquidity than do individual bonds. Plus, you can buy or sell a mutual fund at that day's *net asset value* (NAV) and not have to worry about taking a bad price on a solo bond. By having a professional mutual fund manager on your side, you also pay much less in commission costs than you would as an individual investor. And it is difficult to obtain good research on some bond types, particularly municipal, convertible, and junk bonds. Professionals will always have access to more detailed and timely information than you could get on your own.

Bond mutual funds offer other advantages. If you are an income-oriented investor, a bond fund portfolio can send you a monthly dividend check that will smooth out your cash flow. Individual bonds usually pay every six months, so you may receive a large amount of interest, then have to wait several months before the next payment. If you do not need the cash, bond funds offer automatic dividend reinvestment, which makes it far easier to buy more bonds than waiting for interest to accumulate until you meet the minimum for individual bonds. Finally, a bond fund is made up of tens, if not hundreds, of bonds, diversified by maturity, issuer, and quality. By spreading the risk around, you soften considerably the impact of a negative development on any particular bond. You could not afford such a diversified portfolio on your own, and you are exposed to serious loss if a problem develops with an individual bond.

One disadvantage of bond funds compared with individual bonds is that bond funds (except for zero-coupon bond funds) never mature. Bonds within a portfolio might mature, but the fund is constantly reinvesting the proceeds of matured or sold bonds back into more bonds. This means you have no guarantee that a bond fund will ever return to the price you purchased it at originally. For example, if you buy a fund when interest rates are low and then they rise a great deal, you might have to wait a long time for your principal value to return to where you started. With individual bonds, you can count on a fixed maturity date at which you will receive your original principal. The bond's price will bounce around while it is outstanding, but you can be assured that, in the end, you will get your money back – as long as the issuer does not default.

As with all individual bond prices, bond fund prices move inversely to interest rates. If rates rise, bond fund shares decline in price. As rates fall, bond fund prices rise. If you sell bond fund shares for more than you paid for them, you must pay capital gains tax on the difference. The income you receive from a bond fund is taxable if the fund buys taxable bonds, and it is tax free if the fund invests in municipal securities. To allow bond fund shareholders to keep the taxation of dividends straight, the same bond fund does not buy both taxable and tax-exempt bonds.

As with other kinds of mutual funds, you can choose between no-load bond funds you buy directly from a fund company or load funds you buy indirectly through a broker or financial planner. Loads can have an even bigger effect on your bond fund's return than on a stock fund's return because if the commission is taken off the top, you will have less money earning interest. *12b-1 fees*, which take .5 percent to 1.5 percent of your assets annually, are used for promotional expenses by the fund in order to increase fund assets. Expenses, such as management fees and 12b-1 charges, also have a direct impact on your bond fund's yield. The higher the expenses, the lower the yield. So, as you shop around among bond funds, compare not only the yields but also the effect fees and expense levels will have on your return over time.

Over the last several years, the number and variety of bond funds have mush-roomed, as has the amount of money invested in them. Hundreds of funds now compete for your attention – plus the hundreds of billions of dollars in current total bond fund assets and the billions of dollars more that pour into bond funds each year. And bond fund companies continue to introduce new features already tested on other types of funds.

Two factors distinguish funds: the kinds of securities they buy and the aver-age maturity of the bonds in their portfolios. In general, the longer the fund's portfolio maturity, the higher its yield, and the higher its risk. The following list describes different kinds of bond funds in terms of these two factors.

They have been separated according to the levels of the investment pyramid, from the most conservative to the most aggressive.

Low-Risk Sector

Government bond funds.

Government bond funds invest exclusively in securities issued by the U.S. gov-ernment or its agencies. No risk of default exists in any of the underlying secu-rities; therefore, these are the safest bonds around. Long-term bond funds do carry substantial risk due to interest rate volatility, however.

Municipal bond funds.

These funds invest solely in tax-exempt bonds, so all the dividends they pay are not subject to federal income tax. Depending on your tax bracket, these funds might allow you to keep more interest than you could earn on a higher yielding but taxable bond fund. Three kinds of muni bond funds are available: national, state, and local.

• *National funds* buy bonds from municipalities across the country. In a few cases, interest from a state's bonds is taxable to out-of-state residents, so national bond funds will tell shareholders at the end of the year what percent-age of the income they received came from such a state.

• *State-specific funds* are designed by states for residents of those states who want to avoid both federal and state taxation. Large, high-tax states, such as New York, California, Pennsylvania, and Michigan, offer many single-state funds because so much demand for them exists.

• *Local muni funds* buy bonds only from a locality that levies an income tax, such as New York City. These bonds are therefore triple-tax-free because they allow residents to sidestep federal, state, and local income taxes.

Municipal bond funds are also sold with portfolios composed totally of insured bonds. This insurance protects investors against the possibility of default by any issue a fund holds.

While state and local bond funds offer beneficial tax shelter, they are riskier than national funds because they are not diversified geographically. If a particular state or locality suffers a sharp downturn in its economy, the entity's bonds will probably be downgraded, which could cause shareholders in funds holding those bonds to suffer losses. Still, municipal bond funds, as a whole, are extremely safe; very few defaults have occurred.

Short- and intermediate-term bond funds.

Such funds, which come in both taxable and tax-free varieties, buy bonds with maturities no longer than 10 years, and usually as short as five years. Because short-term bonds fluctuate in price far less than long-term bonds during the same interest rate volatility, these funds' prices remain quite stable. Many short-term funds offer check-writing privileges; therefore, many people use them as higher yielding alternatives to money-market funds. In cases where there exists a significant difference between money-market and medium-term rates, intermediate-term bond funds can offer yields 4 or 5 percentage points higher than money funds. Unlike money funds, however, these funds' *net asset values* (NAVs) fluctuate and will fall if interest rates rise sharply.

Moderate-Risk Sector

Convertible bond funds.

Convertible bond funds buy convertible debentures and convertible preferred stocks. Though convertible yields are lower than those on straight corporate bonds, convertible bond funds offer more appreciation potential. These funds will provide their highest returns when the stock market is rising. The convertible market can be particularly confusing, and a good fund manager's expertise can be well worth the management fee.

High-grade corporate bond funds.

Such funds buy bonds issued by investment-grade corporations, or those with ratings of BBB or higher. The funds will pay yields of 1 or 2 percentage points higher than will government funds of similar maturities. Yet they remain quite safe because they buy top-quality bonds and diversify widely among hundreds of issues.

Mortgage-backed securities funds.

These funds invest in mortgage-backed securities issued by quasi-governmental agencies, such as Ginnie Mae, Fannie Mae, and Freddie Mac. The securities they buy are guaranteed against default by those agencies but not against price fluctuations caused by interest rate movements. The other uncertainty that plagues mortgage-backed securities – the early prepayment of mortgage principal by homeowners – is taken care of by the fund manager, who automatically reinvests principal payments back into more securities. This is a big advantage over holding individual Ginnie Maes or Freddie Macs because it is often difficult to reinvest the small amount of principal paid each month. Mortgage-backed securities funds tend to pay yields of 1 to 3 percentage points higher than similar maturity Treasury funds. Some mortgage-backed funds even permit check writing.

High-Risk Apex

Global bond funds.
Global bond funds purchase bonds issued by governments and corporations from around the world. When interest rates are higher in countries other than the United States, as they were in the early 1990s, these funds can pay yields 2 or 3 percentage points higher than similar domestic funds. What makes them a higher risk is that currency fluctuations can create large swings in the value of fund shares. Because you are, in effect, putting your money in foreign currencies when you buy one of these funds, you will profit if the U.S. dollar falls in value against other currencies. But if the greenback rises in value, you can suffer losses. Some funds try to use complicated futures and options strategies to hedge against currency swings, but the hedges do not always work, and they can be expensive, cutting the funds' yields. The bonds these funds purchase are typically from top-rated governments and corporations, so there is little, if any, default risk. Global bond funds also come in short-term and long-term varieties. Short-term funds usually are less sensitive to currency swings, while long-term funds react more sharply both to interest rate movements and to changes in currency values.

High-yield junk bond funds.
Junk bond funds buy bonds of corporations that are below investment grade, meaning they have ratings of less than BBB. The companies backing these bonds are financially weaker than top-rated blue chip corporations; therefore, the bonds pay higher yields to compensate investors for the increased risk of default. Junk bond funds can pay yields 4 to 6 percentage points higher than government or high-grade corporate bond funds of similar maturities. High-yield fund prices are much more volatile than more conservative bond funds because of rapidly changing values of the bonds they hold. In general, junk

bond funds perform well when the stock market rises because junk bonds mirror the performance of their issuers' stocks.

Zero-coupon bond funds.

Such funds buy portfolios of zero-coupon bonds, which are issued at a deep discount to face value and mature at a specific time in the future. These funds should be considered very conservative if they are held until they liquidate, which occurs when the bonds mature. However, because zero-coupon bonds are the most volatile of all bonds, these funds fluctuate more dramatically than any other kind of bond fund while the bonds are outstanding. Zero-coupon bond funds, which pay no dividends, soar in price when interest rates fall and plunge in price when interest rates rise. If you time your purchases and sales correctly, you can make a lot of money. But if you buy when rates are low and then rates surge, you must hold the funds to maturity to get back your principal.

[Closed-End Bond Funds]

All of the funds described above are open-end funds, meaning that they continually offer new shares to the public as new money flows into the funds. You should also consider shares in closed-end bond funds, which issue a limited number of shares and trade on the NYSE, AMEX, and Nasdaq NMS.

Closed-end bond funds, like all closed-end funds, sell at either a premium or a discount to the current value of their bond portfolios. They typically sell at a premium to, or for more than, the portfolios' value when interest rates decline and investors scramble into closed-end bond funds in search of higher yields. But when interest rates rise, fund prices tend to shrink to a discount.

A good strategy is to buy closed-end bond funds when they are at a discount because this will boost your yield. To calculate your effective yield, divide the annual dividend by the current price of the fund. For example, assume that a bond fund pays a $.70 annual dividend, and the NAV of the fund's portfolio – or the exact worth of its portfolio – is $10 per share. If the fund is selling at its NAV, its effective yield is 7 percent.

$$\frac{\$.70 \text{ Annual dividend}}{\$10 \text{ Current price of the fund}} = 7\% \text{ Effective yield}$$

If investors temporarily lose confidence in the fund and its price falls to $9, it is selling at a 10 percent discount. Because the annual dividend remains at $.70, the effective yield will rise to 7.77 percent.

$$\frac{\$.70 \text{ Annual dividend}}{\$9 \text{ Current price of the fund}} = 7.77\% \text{ Effective yield}$$

If investors become enthusiastic about the fund again and its price rises to $11, it is selling at a 10 percent premium. Therefore, the effective yield will fall to 6.36 percent.

$$\frac{\$.70 \text{ Annual dividend}}{\$11 \text{ Current price of the fund}} = 6.36\% \text{ Effective yield}$$

While it is easy enough to calculate the effective yields of closed-end funds, you can also look up these payouts in financial newspapers like *The Wall Street Journal* (on Mondays) and *Barron's*. They will list each bond fund's current price, NAV, and effective yield. You can also find the price and yield in NYSE, AMEX, and Nasdaq NMS tables because closed-end funds trade through these systems.

Closed-end bond funds, like their open-end cousins, come in both general and specialized categories. General funds can invest in any kind of bond that the fund's manager thinks will produce capital gains and income. These funds might have a combination of government, municipal, corporate, foreign, convertible, junk, and zero-coupon bonds, as well as mortgage-backed securities, in their portfolios. Their wide diversification makes them less risky than specialized funds, which buy only one type of those bonds listed above. Still, a specialized fund might yield higher income if it invests only in tax-free municipal bonds or in high-yielding junk bonds, for example.

[U n i t   I n v e s t m e n t   T r u s t s]

Instead of buying an open-end or a closed-end bond fund, you have another alternative if you are income-oriented. *Unit investment trusts* (UITs), sometimes called *defined asset trusts*, buy a fixed portfolio of bonds and hold them to maturity. These contrast with bond funds, which constantly buy and sell bonds and never mature.

You can buy a UIT from any broker for a minimum of $1,000. You usually pay a sales charge of about 4 percent or 5 percent when you buy it, then minimal management expenses thereafter of .15 percent per year. The underwriter of the portfolio also profits by marking up the bonds it buys for the portfolio. Over the long term, though, these fees are less than the typical annual management fees of 1 percent or more on more actively managed bond funds. A few large brokerage firms, including Merrill Lynch, Nuveen, and Van Kampen Merritt, dominate the UIT business. The trusts are usually sold through syndicates of brokerage firms that unite to sell one trust after another.

UITs offer several advantages.

• You buy into a widely diversified, professionally selected portfolio that would be impossible to replicate on your own.

• You know exactly what assets the trust contains before you buy it. That is why they are called defined asset trusts.

• You receive fixed monthly income checks, as opposed to payments every six months from individual bonds.

• If you need access to your capital, you can sell your units back to the sponsoring company, though you might have to sell at a discount.

• You receive your principal back when the portfolio of bonds matures (usually in about 20 years), unlike a bond fund, which never matures.

• You can choose a UIT that fits your income needs. Many trusts specialize in municipal bonds and therefore pay tax-free interest. Within that category, some trusts buy only bonds from a particular state, yielding double-tax-free income. For investors who want extra security, other municipal trusts buy only insured bonds. In addition to municipal bonds, UITs buy mortgage-backed securities, high-quality corporate bonds, foreign bonds, and even junk bonds.

Because they own fixed portfolios of bonds, UITs can get hurt if there is a problem with some of the bonds in their portfolios. For example, in the early 1980s, a consortium of municipalities that had banded together to build nuclear power plants in Washington state (called the Washington Public Power Supply System and commonly known as WHOOPS) defaulted on billions of dollars in bonds, many of which were held in UIT portfolios. While some of the bonds were insured, leaving trustholders unaffected, others were not. Thus, many UITs suffered losses and had to reduce monthly payouts. In extreme cases, UIT managers can sell bonds if they sense trouble coming, but such active management is the exception. When bonds are sold, however, the principal is returned to UIT holders because UITs are not allowed to add new bonds to a portfolio once it has been sold.

When shopping for a UIT, look carefully at the prospectus describing the portfolio. Notice the average maturity of the bonds, which may range from 10 years to as many as 30 years. Inspect the bonds' safety ratings, making sure that they fall in the A category if you want to depend on the trust for income for many years. Determine what kind of call protection comes with the bonds in the portfolio. Ideally, you would like at least 10 years before the bonds can be redeemed.

With a little homework, you may find a UIT that meets your needs for dependable monthly income.

[FIVE]

Speculating with Futures and Options

[The Basics of Futures Trading]

Despite the enormous risks of futures trading, the tremendous potential for quick profits attracts thousands of new investors to the markets every year.

A *futures contract* is an obligation to buy or sell a specific quantity of a commodity, financial instrument, or stock index at a fixed price at a particular date in the future. Buying a contract obligating you to take delivery of the underlying commodity is known as *taking a long position.* For example, you might buy a futures contract obligating you to accept delivery of 100 troy ounces of gold for $350 on June 20. This particular contract is available on the Chicago Board of Trade (CBOT). If you were to follow through on the contract and buy all the gold, it would cost you $35,000 ($350 x 100 ounces).

The profit potential – and danger – of futures trading stems from the fact that you must put up only a small percentage, usually between 5 percent and 10 percent, of the contract's value to play the game. This money, a form of good faith deposit, is known as *margin.* In the example, if you had to put up 5 percent, it would cost you $1,750 to control the $35,000 contract.

As the price of the underlying commodity rises or falls, the worth of your contract surges or plunges. For example, if the price of gold rises from $350 to $400, the value of the underlying contract would soar to $40,000. Your profit would be $5,000 because the contract you bought that was worth $35,000 is now worth $40,000. Of course, if you had bought 10 contracts, you would have earned a $50,000 profit.

On the other hand, if gold fell from \$350 to \$332.50, you would have lost all your \$1,750 deposit money. If gold prices dropped from \$332.50 to a lower price, your broker would send you a *margin call* (i.e., more money to cover your additional losses above and beyond your original \$1,750 deposit). If gold dropped to \$300, you would need an additional \$3,250 to maintain your market position. If you don't meet the margin call, the contract would be liquidated immediately. If you do meet the margin call, you would maintain your position in the futures contract. When the delivery date arrives, you would have to buy \$35,000 worth of gold, which would then be worth only \$30,000, thus saddling you with a \$5,000 loss per contract. If you were the seller of this contract, you would not have to worry about losing money if the buyer cuts his or her losses and runs – or even skips town. The commodity brokerage firm and, ultimately, the commodity exchange on which the trade was made, guarantee that the buyer's obligations will be met.

If you believe that the price of the underlying commodity will fall, you can sell a futures contract short, or take a *short position*. The previous example would then work in reverse: You would profit if the price of the commodity fell and lose money if the commodity's price rose.

Another, more conservative, way to play futures is to buy or sell what is known as a *spread*. Instead of taking a pure bet that a commodity's price will rise if you are a buyer or fall if you are a seller, you can play both sides of a trade and profit by the spread widening or narrowing. For example, you might buy a long gold contract for one month and sell short another gold contract for another month. The spread between the price from one month to another would widen or narrow over time, giving you the chance to profit. Or you can spread one commodity against a similar one and hope to profit from the differential. For instance, you might buy a gold contract for one month and sell a silver contract for the same month, trying to profit from a change in the relationship between gold and silver.

While, in theory, you could actually accept delivery of the underlying commodity by taking possession of the 100 troy ounces of gold (to use the previous example), almost no one does. Only about 1 percent of futures contracts traded are settled by delivery, and that is done at a designated warehouse designed to transfer ownership of commodities. Most contracts are liquidated long before they expire. To cancel a contract, you would close out your position by taking the opposite side, netting you either a profit or a loss. In the earlier example, if you had gone long by buying a contract for gold, you could close out your position by selling the contract. Investing in futures is known as a *zero-sum game* because for every contract that profits, someone holds an offsetting contract that loses.

If you are thinking of playing the futures game, keep these guidelines in mind:

• *Play only with money you can afford to lose.* Don't speculate with money you need to rely on to cover your mortgage payment or your child's tuition.

• *Figure out in advance at what level you would promise yourself to take a profit or at what price you would promise to cut your losses.* This is important because the futures game can get you so entangled psychologically that you lose all perspective. Many people have seen profits slip from their grasp as they became greedy to earn even more. Others have stubbornly refused to cut their mushrooming losses on the foolish conviction that "the market will come around to my way of thinking." One way to impose this discipline on yourself is to set an automatic level at which you sell to capture a profit and an automatic stop-loss level at which your losses will be limited to a predetermined amount.

• *Don't assume you will win with every trade.* If you continue to cut your losses so they do not get out of hand, you will be in a position to let your profits run when you hit a big winner.

• *Figure in the costs of brokerage commissions in assessing your chances for profits or losses.* Brokers love futures trading because it involves so many transactions, each of which generates a commission. The costs of overtrading have sunk many investors.

• *Leave a cash cushion in your futures account* so that if the market goes against you, you do not have to scramble to come up with cash to meet a margin call.

• *Understand what you are getting into before you invest any money.* Work with an experienced broker, and study the factors that influence a particular market and what has happened in that market recently. Also, before you actually invest money, you could try some hypothetical trading. However you learn about futures, don't hurry to get into futures trading; the markets will be there whenever you decide you're ready.

Futures Pools and Discretionary Accounts

If you're not able to devote the time and emotional energy involved in trading futures (that includes most investors!), you have two ways to let professional futures traders do the work for you. First, you can invest in a futures pool, which is similar to a mutual fund. Investors pool millions of dollars with an established futures money management firm, which then buys and sells contracts in many different markets simultaneously, including agricultural, financial, industrial, metal, and foreign currency futures.

Two advantages of participating in these pools are that you have a professional money manager watching your positions at all times, and you will never be subject to a margin call. If the manager runs into a serious losing streak, the pool may be dissolved earlier than anticipated, and you may get back only part of your principal. If everything goes well, on the other hand, the pool will be liquidated in five or 10 years, and all profits will be distributed to pool participants, minus the fees that have been deducted every year. These fees, which amount to as much as 6 percent of managed assets each year, are charged on top of brokerage commissions of as much as 10 percent of your capital. In addition, the management company may take up to a 30 percent incentive fee from the fund's new profits. Unlike stock and bond mutual funds, it is not easy to get out of a futures pool once you have invested in one. Most brokerage firms require you to keep your capital in the pool at least three, and usually six, months.

The performance of these pools varies widely from pool to pool and year to year. They do best when the markets move sharply upward or downward and the pools are invested on the correct side of the move. They tend to do little when the markets are placid. And if they are on the wrong side of a market move, they can lose a lot of money in a hurry. Most brokerage firms sell participations in futures pools. You can size up an offering by looking at the futures manager's track record; however, that is no guarantee of future performance. Brokers want to sell to managers with hot records, and what worked before may not work again as the fast-moving markets change.

The best way to follow the performance of different money managers and the pools they manage is to subscribe to *Managed Account Reports* (220 Fifth Ave., 19th Floor, New York, NY 10001; 212-213-6202). This rating service provides monthly updates and industry averages for futures pools. In addition, several firms track the performance of futures money managers and will place your money with the top managers. One such firm is A.T.A. Research (5910 N. Central Expressway, Suite 1520, Dallas, TX 75206; 214-373-7606).

The second way to let professional futures traders invest your money for you is to sign up for a discretionary account with a futures trading adviser. Such an account gives a professional trader full discretion to buy and sell futures contracts without your prior authorization. The adviser receives an annual management fee of about 2 percent of your capital. In many cases, the trading adviser will also take an annual percentage – up to about 20 percent – of any profits he or she generates. You must be extremely careful in signing up for such an account, no matter how brilliant the track record of the trading adviser. Once he or she has your money and your signature on the dotted line, you have no power to stop the adviser's trading activity unless you revoke the agreement altogether.

Many brokerage firms will recommend futures trading advisers with good records. You can also contact the Managed Futures Association (P.O. Box 287, Palo Alto, CA 94302; 415-325-4533).

[The Basics of Options Trading]

Though they are also speculative, options have one advantage over futures: The amount of money you can lose is limited to the amount of money you invested in the option. In futures, remember, you can actually lose more than you invest if you are hit with a margin call. While this limited-loss feature of options may provide some comfort, it doesn't change the fact that you can lose every penny of your investment.

Options come in two varieties: a *call* and a *put*. You buy a call when you think the underlying stock, stock index, or futures contract will rise in value, and you buy a put when you think the underlying investment will fall in value. Following is an explanation of how each works.

Calls.

When you buy a *call option*, you receive the right, but not the obligation, to buy a stock, an index, or a futures contract at a set price for a particular period of time, usually a few months. For example, you might purchase the right to buy General Motors stock at $35 a share from now until February 20, which, let us say, is about a month from now. The person who sells you the option, known as the *option writer*, receives in return a nonrefundable payment called a *premium.* In this case, the premium might be $4 a share, or $300 total, because options are traded in minimums of 100 shares.

Assume that when you buy it, GM stock is trading at $38 a share. You are about even because your option gives you the right to buy at $35, and you paid $4 for the option. If GM stock shoots up from $38 to $45, or 18 percent, in the next month, your option's price will rocket from $4 to $10 – a 150 percent gain. You could now do one of two things. First, you could exercise your right to buy 100 shares of GM stock at $35 a share for $3,500, then sell it in the open market for $45 a share, or $4,500 total, pocketing a $10-per-share, or $1,000, gain. Alternatively, you could sell the option for $10 per share, or $1,000 total, taking home a $600 gain ($1,000 minus the original $400 you paid for the premium). Most of the time, investors sell the option for a profit and do not actually exercise their right to buy the underlying shares.

If, instead of shooting up to $45 per share, however, GM stock either remains the same or falls, your option would expire worthless on February 20. You would lose your entire $400 premium.

Puts.

When you buy a put, you want the underlying investment to fall in price – exactly the opposite of what you want to happen when you buy a call. A put gives you the right, but not the obligation, to sell a stock, an index, or a futures contract at a set price for a particular period of time, usually a few months. If you think General Motors stock is about to fall in price, for instance, you could buy a General Motors put giving you the right to sell General Motors stock at $35 a share any time over the next month to February 20. With GM stock at $38, that right might cost you a premium of only ¼ of a point, or $25 (100 shares times .25).

If GM stock plummets from $38 to $30 over the next month, a 21 percent decline, your put would soar in value from ¼ to $5, or 19 times your premium investment. You could now do one of two things. You could exercise your option by selling General Motors stock at $35 per share for $3,500, then buy it back on the open market for $30 a share, or $3,000 total, and pocket the $500 difference. Or you could sell your option for $5 per share, or $500 total, and walk off with a $475 profit ($500 minus your $25 premium).

On the other hand, if GM stock either remains the same or rises in price before February 20, your put would expire worthless. You would lose your $25 premium.

As you can see, profits or losses in options can be significant and achieved in a short amount of time. If you buy a call or a put, the underlying investment must move up or down far enough and fast enough for you to make a profit. If you buy a call and the stock moves up, but not before your option expires, you still lose.

A key factor in whether you profit in options is the price of the premium. This price is determined by several factors, including the general direction of the underlying investment, the volatility level of the underlying investment, and the time remaining before the option expires. Options are known as *wasting assets*, meaning that they waste away as time goes on. If you buy an option, time is your enemy because the option is worth less and less each day. If you sell an option, time is your friend because you want the option to expire without being exercised.

As with futures, you can hedge your bets with options by buying combinations of options called *spreads* or *straddles*. You can buy a call option with one date, like February, and a put option with another date, like April, and hope to profit from the change in the relationship between the two. Or you can buy a call on gold, for instance, and a put on silver and, again, hope to profit as the difference between the two options widens or narrows.

Another way to play options is to sell them on your existing holdings instead of buying them on investments you don't own. This is known as *writing covered options.* For example, say you own 100 shares of General Motors stock. If you write, or sell, a call option when the stock is at $38 a share, you will receive $4 a share, or $400 total, in premium, which is yours to keep no matter what happens to GM's stock price. (The $4 a share is a function of the bullishness or bearishness of the marketplace, time remaining in the option's life, as well as several other factors.) If the price goes up enough, you might have to sell your stock to the option buyer because that is a right you grant when you sell the option. If, on the other hand, GM stock doesn't move or even goes down, you keep your stock and the $400 premium. Therefore, writing options can be a conservative strategy to boost the income you receive from a stock in addition to its dividends.

As long as you own the underlying shares and are able to deliver them if the option is exercised, selling options is a rather conservative strategy because you know in advance the worst that can happen: You would have to sell your shares to the option buyer at the predetermined price. In the previous example, that means you would receive a $400 premium and $35 a share, or $3,500, for your stock. You would not feel too happy, however, if the shares rose to $45 or more because you would no longer own the stock.

Daredevils in the options market sell options without owning the underlying shares, a strategy known as "naked" option writing. If the stock's price remains fixed or falls, someone who has sold a call for a $400 premium can keep the cash without having invested any money. However, if the stock price shoots up, the investor must buy shares in the market at the higher price to be able to deliver shares when the option is exercised. Most investors shouldn't try naked options writing until they are quite knowledgeable about the options market – and probably not even then.

You can pursue many strategies in the options market, from the very conservative to the extremely aggressive. As in futures, the excitement of potential profits can lure you into taking more risk than you probably should. Therefore, study the options market carefully before you invest.

[SIX]

Other Investments:
Gold and Real Estate

[Gold and Other Precious Metals]

ince 3000 B.C., gold has been recognized as the ultimate medium of exchange. Because gold is rare, in continuous demand, and portable, it is considered the supreme store of value. In contrast, paper money, printed by governments, can be eroded by inflation or the collapse of those governments. Gold is an asset in its own right; it does not require a government, a corporation or any other entity to validate it. For example, when Vietnam was falling to the Communists in 1975, Vietnamese refugees weren't interested in escaping with South Vietnamese currency; it would be worthless. They fled with gold coins and bars, which they knew would have value wherever they ended up.

Is there a place for gold in your investment portfolio? The answer depends on your outlook for inflation and the total mix of your portfolio.

Traditionally, gold has been seen as a hedge not only against high inflation but also against high international tension. This was certainly true during the 1970s, when gold shot up dramatically in a day based on the latest rumors of war in the Middle East or in some other part of the world. But over the past few years, gold seems to have lost its appeal even during times of turmoil. Despite such dramatic events in the late 1980s and early 1990s as the collapse of Communism and the related outbreaks of ethnic tension throughout the former Soviet empire, the Persian Gulf War, the strife in Yugoslavia, and the world-wide recession, gold hardly budged from the $325 to $450 trading range. This was because inflation remained well under control, and investors did not feel the need to hedge themselves against rising prices as they had in the late 1970s.

Though it seems unlikely that a repeat of the 1970s inflation and gold price surge will occur, gold may still have a role to play in your investment portfolio. Studies show that over the long term, portfolios containing gold are more stable and have higher returns than gold-free portfolios because gold tends to move in the opposite direction of paper assets, such as stocks and bonds. This counter-weight effect – again, over the long term – provides protection against unforeseen events, even though in the short term gold holdings may severely under-perform stocks and bonds.

All this holds true for other precious metals as well, though to a lesser degree. Silver and platinum are also used by investors as inflation hedges, but they are not seen as the ultimate store of value, as is gold. Gold is used in the jewelry, dentistry, and electronics industries; however, its price is determined mainly by the supply from gold mines and by investment demand, not as much by industrial factors. The other precious metals have wider industrial uses – silver in photography, electrical and electronics, jewelry, and silverware; diamonds in jewelry and as cutting tools; and platinum and palladium in jewelry and catalytic converters for automobiles. These metals tend to fluctuate in price based more on industrial supply and demand than on investment demand (see Figure 25).

Investing in precious metals is, by its nature, risky. Most forms of metals investing do not provide income, so you depend totally on an increase in the metal's price in order to profit. While profits can be enormous at certain times in the economic cycle, metals prices may remain depressed for several years in a row and yield little or no return. Most investment advisers recommend that you invest between 5 percent and 10 percent of your portfolio in one form of gold, silver, or platinum to serve as a long-term hedge.

Investors looking to hedge their portfolios with gold and other precious metals have five principal ways of participating in the markets: coins and bars; certificates; shares in precious-metals-mining companies; mutual funds that buy precious metals-mining stocks; and futures and options on gold, silver, and platinum.

Coins and Bars

The most convenient and direct way to invest in the precious-metals markets is to buy coins and bars that have been minted specifically for investors. Coins fall into two categories: *bullion* and *numismatic*. Bars are always bullion. Bullion coins and bars are pure or near-pure gold, silver or platinum, and therefore trade almost solely on their metal content. Numismatic coins are minted in limited quantities, sometimes for a specific event, like the Olympics or the coronation of a king. They trade on supply and demand for the specific coin and on the artistic traits and condition of the coin.

Fig. 25 Platinum Typically Trades at a Premium to Gold

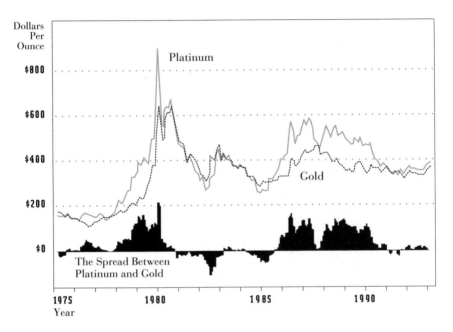

Source: Adapted used by permission of Platinum Guild International (USA) Inc. (Nearby Contract; Avg. Monthly Close).

The Case for Bullion

For investment purposes, you should stick with bullion coins and bars. They trade for a small markup of from 1 percent to 15 percent more than the price of the underlying metal. Gold coins and bars come in many sizes, from a one-gram bar or a 1/25-ounce coin to a one-ounce coin (a one-kilo coin by the Australian mint is the exception) to a 400-ounce bar. Don't expect to find one of these large bars, which would be worth $160,000 if gold were $400 an ounce, in your local coin dealer's front window, however. They are normally used by central banks and governments to settle debts. If you're interested, you can see several hundred of them in the vault at the Federal Reserve in New York City or at Fort Knox, Kentucky.

The best size coin to purchase is the one-ounce variety because it is easiest to buy and sell. Many countries produce one-ounce gold coins, but the most popular (in alphabetical order by country) are the Australian Nugget, the

Austrian Philharmonica, the British Britannia, the Canadian Maple Leaf, the Mexican Peso, the South African Krugerrand, and the U.S. Gold Eagle. As part of the now lifted apartheid-related ban on South African products, no new Krugerrands were imported into the United States for years, though an active secondary market in Krugerrands still exists worldwide.

Among one-ounce silver coins, the most popular are the Australian Kookaburra, the Canadian Silver Maple Leaf, and the U.S. Silver Eagle. Silver can also be purchased in bags of coins worth about $1,000 per bag and bars of many sizes ranging from one ounce to 1,000 ounces. Silver usually sells for far less per ounce than gold and might therefore be more affordable for starting bullion investors.

Platinum coins usually sell for more than either gold or silver because platinum is rarer. The most popular one-ounce platinum coins are the Australian Koala Bear, the Canadian Platinum Maple Leaf, and the Isle of Man Noble. So few palladium coins circulate that they are not worth buying for investment purposes.

When buying bullion coins, you should shop around among coin dealers, banks, and brokerage houses because they all charge slightly different markups or sales charges. Because many fly-by-night coin dealers charge excessive markups, it is best to associate with a dealer who is a member of the Professional Numismatists Guild (P.O. Box 430, Van Nuys, CA 91408; 818-781-1764), which holds its members to high ethical standards. Be particularly wary of dealers who solicit you over the phone but have no office nearby. Many stories circulate about firms that set up shop, deliver high-pressure sales pitches promising huge instant profits, collect investors' money, then disappear as quickly as they appeared. Another safe way to buy coins is through coin conventions or shows, where you haggle with other investors over prices. You can find out about such shows from the American Numismatic Association (818 N. Cascade Ave., Colorado Springs, CO 80903; 719-632-2646).

If you build up a sizable collection of bullion coins, keep them in a secure place, preferably a safe-deposit box, even though this adds to your cost of owning the coins. You might also consider a rider on your home insurance policy to cover theft of your coins if you insist on keeping them at home.

If you want to buy bars instead of coins, you can choose among more than 19 sizes and weights, from the tiny one-gram to the one-ounce, five-ounce, 10-ounce and kilo bar, which equals 32.15 troy ounces. Bars are usually engraved with the name of the company that created them. When you buy, look for the most recognized names: Englehard Metals, Johnson Matthey, and Credit Suisse. Bars are generally sealed in a plastic container to protect them from scratching and chipping. If your bars have been removed from their plastic, or they are marked with an unfamiliar company name, the dealer you want to sell them to may require that the bars be assayed, or weighed and inspected, to make sure they are acceptable. This process will cost you up to 1 percent of the bars' price, which will cut into your return.

Certificates

If you want to invest in precious metals for profit and don't care about holding the metal itself, a certificate may be the best thing to buy. A gold, silver, platinum or palladium certificate represents ownership of a particular amount of metal, which is stored in a bank vault. Certificates are sold in minimum lots of $1,000 by banks, brokerage firms and coin dealers at commissions ranging from 1 percent to 3 percent of the purchase price, depending on the size of the order. When you cash in your certificate, the bank or broker will usually charge a 1 percent sales commission. In addition, the bank holding the metal will charge an annual storage and insurance fee of up to another percentage point of the certificate's value. But make sure that you deal only with reputable companies.

Precious-Metals Stocks

An even more volatile way to ride the ups and downs of the gold, silver, and platinum markets is to invest in publicly traded mining companies. Their stocks, like all stocks, rise and fall based on investors' expectations of future profits. This means that investors' projections of higher or lower gold and silver prices, or hopes that a new "mother lode" gold mine will be found, can cause sharp increases or decreases in a mining company's stock price. Gold mining shares usually shoot up faster and fall more sharply than gold bullion prices.

Two kinds of gold-mining shares exist: North American-Australian mine issues and South African mine issues. North American-Australian mines tend to pay lower dividends than South African mines and are influenced more by developments at the company. South African issues are frequently affected by political turmoil and labor strikes in South Africa, as well as by fluctuations in the value of the South African rand against the U.S. dollar. It might be possible, for instance, that strife in South Africa that threatens to shut down gold mines would cause the price of gold to soar because the markets fear a gold shortage, while South African gold-mining shares would plunge because of the mines' lost production.

North American-Australian mining shares, on the other hand, can rise in price even if the price of gold is stagnant or falling slightly. Improved technology often allows some companies to extract more gold from their mines, so the firms' profits will rise because of increased output. You have plenty of solid, well-known North American mining companies to choose from, such as American Barrick Resources, Newmont Mining, and Homestake Mining, all traded on the New York Stock Exchange (NYSE). Don't be tempted by small, penny-stock firms that hope to strike it rich someday. They are far too risky an investment for your hard-earned capital.

If you want to invest in even riskier platinum and palladium, you can buy shares in two South African companies – Rustenberg Platinum and Impala Mines, both available in the form of American depositary receipts (ADRs). Remember, though, that these shares are subject to the volatility of the South African political situation.

Precious-Metals Mutual Funds

A safer way to invest in gold- and silver-mining stocks is to buy shares in one of the many *open-ended mutual funds* that specialize in precious metals. Because they invest in mining stocks, the funds tend to be more volatile than the price of bullion, but because they are diversified, the funds are safer than investing all your money in one stock. Like all mutual funds, precious-metals funds are run by a professional manager who dedicates all his or her time to analyzing mining stocks. Some funds specifically avoid South African gold-mining companies, while others mix South African, North American, and Australian shares. These mutual funds pay dividends, which can easily be reinvested in more shares.

The following are the largest and best-performing precious-metals mutual funds, with their national toll-free telephone numbers, followed by their in-state telephone numbers, if available.

Benham Gold Equities Index Fund; 800-472-3389; 800-321-8321

Blanchard Precious Metals Fund; 800-922-7771; 212-779-7979

Bull & Bear Gold Investors Limited; 800-847-4200; 212-363-1100

Colonial Advanced Strategies Gold; 800-426-3750

Dean Witter Precious Metals; 800-869-3863

Excel Midas Gold Shares & Bullion; 800-333-9235; 619-485-9400

Fidelity Select American Gold Fund; 800-544-6666

Fidelity Select Precious Metals and Minerals; 800-544-6666

Financial Strategic Gold Fund; 800-525-8085; 303-779-1233

Franklin Gold Fund; 800-342-5236; 415-570-3000

Freedom Gold & Government; 800-225-6258

IDS Precious Metals Fund; 800-328-8300; 612-372-3733

International Investors; 800-221-2220; 212-687-5201

Kemper Gold Fund; 800-621-1148

Keystone Precious Metals Fund; 800-633-4900

Lexington Goldfund; 800-526-0056

Mainstay Gold and Precious Metals Fund; 800-522-4202

MFS Lifetime Gold & Precious Metals; 800-225-2606; 617-954-5000

Monitrend Gold Fund; 800-251-1970; 615-298-1000

Oppenheimer Gold & Special Minerals Fund; 800-255-2755

Pioneer Gold Shares; 800-225-6292; 617-742-7825

Rushmore Precious Metals Index; 800-343-3355; 301-657-1500

Scudder Gold Fund; 800-225-2470

Shearson Precious Metals & Minerals Fund; 800-451-2010; 212-720-9218

Shearson Precious Metals Portfolio; 800-451-2010; 212-720-9218

Strategic Gold and Minerals Fund; 800-526-0056

Strategic Investments Fund; 800-526-0056

Strategic Silver Fund; 800-526-0056

Thomson Precious Metals A; 800-628-1237; 212-482-5984

Thomson Precious Metals B; 800-628-1237; 212-482-5984

United Gold & Government; 800-366-5465

United Services Global Resources; 800-873-8637

United Services Gold Shares; 800-873-8637

United Services World Gold Fund; 800-873-8637

USAA Investment Trust: Gold; 800-531-8181; 512-498-4499

Van Eck Gold Resources; 800-221-2220; 212-687-5200

Van Eck International Investors; 800-221-2220; 212-687-5200

Vanguard Specialized Gold & Precious Metals; 800-662-7447

You have two options among *closed-end funds* for investing in gold and silver. One is called the Central Fund of Canada (P.O. Box 7319, Ancaster, Ontario, Canada L9G 3N6; 416-648-7878), and it trades on the American Stock Exchange (AMEX). The fund owns a large cache of gold and silver bullion, which it keeps in a bank vault. This fund therefore offers no risk of exploration or production of gold. It is as pure an investment in bullion as you can get without holding the metal in your hands.

The other closed-end fund is ASA Limited (P.O. Box 269, Florham Park, NJ 07932; 201-377-3535). This fund invests almost exclusively in shares of South African mining companies and is therefore subject to all the ups and downs of the South African market and the fluctuations of the South African rand against the U.S. dollar.

[I n v e s t m e n t   R e a l   E s t a t e]

Buying a home is the primary, but by no means the only, way to profit from real estate. Investing in real estate for profit is tricky and can take a great deal of time and expertise. Real estate has the advantages of appreciation potential, rental income, and tax benefits. On the other hand, it can be extremely illiquid (hard to sell), and management-intensive. The real estate market is also subject to the influence of national trends, such as changes in tax laws and interest rates, as well as local trends in economic growth and supply and demand for similar properties.

When seeking advice about investing in real estate, make sure that you know whom you listen to. The field is rife with self-promoters promising instant riches for no money down. Their so-called seminars are, in fact, high-pressure sales pitches. These scam artists usually show off their wealth to impress you; however, they have probably earned their millions by *giving* bad real estate advice, not *taking* it. Some tout enormous riches to be made in foreclosed property. Others guarantee wealth through government loan programs. A few want you to believe your road to easy street is paved with *multilevel marketing*, another term for a pyramid or Ponzi scheme. Be extremely careful when dealing with these promoters. Their presentations are slick and convincing, but the chances that you will end up as rich as they are slim or nonexistent.

If you wish to invest legitimately in real estate, you have seven principal ways to do so. They are ranked and discussed below from the safest to the most speculative: real estate mutual funds; real estate investment trusts; real estate limited partnerships; rental real estate; vacation homes; timeshares; and raw land.

Real Estate Mutual Funds

Several mutual funds invest in publicly traded real estate-oriented stocks. As do all mutual funds, they provide a widely diversified portfolio of securities, professional management, and reasonable management fees of about 1 percent of your assets each year. Because many of these funds buy real estate investment trusts (REITs) that pay high dividends, the funds can pay yields of 2 percent to about 5 percent. In addition to REITs, these funds buy stocks of home builders and suppliers to the home-building industry.

Real estate funds tend to perform well when interest rates fall and when occupancy and rental rates rise. Conversely, they tend to underperform during periods of rising interest rates and when gluts of real estate exist on the market. Some funds buy only U.S. real estate companies, while other global funds invest in real estate companies around the world.

Four of the best real estate mutual funds are Evergreen Global Real Estate (800-235-0064); Fidelity Real Estate (800-544-8888); Templeton Real Estate (800-237-0738); and United Services Real Estate (800-873-8637). Evergreen and Templeton are global real estate funds.

Real Estate Investment Trusts (REITs)

REITs are publicly traded stocks that invest in office buildings, apartment complexes, industrial facilities, shopping centers, and other commercial spaces. Under current law, they do not pay taxes at the corporate level as long as they distribute at least 95 percent of their earnings to shareholders in the form of dividends each year. Shareholders then pay taxes on the dividends as regular income. In some cases, a portion of the dividends may be considered a return of capital for tax purposes and, therefore, is not taxed.

Three primary types of REITs exist:

Equity.

These trusts buy properties, fix them up, collect rents, and sometimes sell the properties at a profit. Equity REIT share prices greatly reflect the general direction of real estate values. Some equity REITs buy different kinds of properties across the country. Others specialize in a particular type of real estate. For example, several REITs, including Meditrust (128 Technology Center,

Waltham, MA 02154; 617-736-1500) and Health Care REIT, Inc. (One Seagate, Suite 1950, P.O. Box 1475, Toledo, OH 43603; 419-247-2800), concentrate on health care facilities. Others buy properties in one region of the country. For example, Washington REIT (10400 Connecticut Ave., Concourse Level, Kensington, MD 20895; 301-929-5900) buys properties in the Washington, D.C., market, while Weingarten Realty Investors (2600 Citadel Plaza Dr., Suite 300, Houston, TX 77708; 713-866-6000) specializes in shopping centers in Texas and Louisiana. Equity REITs can provide some protection against inflation because they usually include rent escalator clauses in their contracts with tenants so that price increases can be passed along in the form of higher rents.

Mortgage.
This form of REIT originates or buys mortgages on commercial properties. Mortgage REITs offer yields of about 6 percent to 10 percent – much more than the 4 percent to 7 percent paid by equity REITs. But mortgage REITs offer little capital appreciation potential. If mortgages get into trouble or default, share prices can plunge.

Hybrid.
These REITs combine equity and mortgage holdings. Hybrid trusts pay yields of 6 percent to 9 percent and offer some appreciation potential.

The REIT industry has become notorious for a boom and bust cycle. Its first boom occurred in the early 1970s, which led to an enormous bust in the 1973–1974 recession, when many REITs went bankrupt in the wake of massive overbuilding. The industry recovered and prospered for much of the 1980s until the real estate market again became glutted in the late 1980s and early 1990s. In the early 1990s, REIT shares were popular again as lower interest rates and tightening rental markets in many places across the country boosted share prices.

Real Estate Limited Partnerships

Limited partnerships (LPs), which saw their heyday in the 1980s, raise money from limited partners and invest it in new or existing commercial real estate. Decisions on what to buy and how to manage the properties are made by a general partner.

Unlike real estate funds or REITs, LPs are not easy to buy and sell. When you buy, you must pay onerous sales charges and other fees that may amount to as much as 10 percent of your invested capital. On top of that, you remit annual management fees of 2 percent or 3 percent of your principal. If you want to withdraw from the partnership before it is liquidated, which occurs up to 10 years after its launch, you must sell in a tricky secondary market where investors offer to buy your units at deep discounts.

In theory, a good real estate partnership produces high current income from rents and mortgage interest it collects. Upon liquidation, partners receive magnificent capital gains when the partnership's properties are sold for huge profits. The reality of the past decade has been far from the hype, as many partnerships have suffered defaults, plunging property values and declining rental income.

Another form of real estate partnership that offers more liquidity is a *master limited partnership* (MLP). These operate just like traditional partnerships except that they trade on exchanges like any other stock. In some cases, an MLP has been formed by combining the assets of several troubled illiquid partnerships into one giant, publicly traded vehicle. MLPs typically pay high dividends of 5 percent to 10 percent.

Rental Real Estate

Becoming a landlord has its advantages and disadvantages. If you own a good property, it can appreciate handsomely over time and provide solid rental income. In addition, you can reap substantial tax benefits, such as writing off losses up to $25,000 against other income, if you meet certain IRS restrictions.

On the other hand, few people think being a landlord is fun. Tenants often complain. You are responsible if the plumbing breaks down in the middle of the night or the heat shuts off in the dead of winter. Not every renter pays his or her rent on time. You must constantly guard against vandalism. You must sometimes evict a tenant. And in some localities, rent controls prevent you from raising rents enough to cover increased expenses.

The key to successful rental real estate is to buy properties in good locations that attract the type of tenant who takes care of his or her unit and is so happy living on the property that he or she never objects to rent hikes every year. Easier said than done!

When looking for profitable rental properties, you might begin in working-class neighborhoods, where prices are more reasonable and tenants more reliable than they are in the elite neighborhoods of town. To find a bargain, you could focus on properties with problems that are relatively easy to resolve. The problem – be it asbestos, a leaky roof, or some other repair – might scare the current owner so much that he or she will sell at a large discount from the property's real value. Before buying, determine how much it will cost to resolve the problem, and estimate the rent you could collect once the place is in tip-top shape.

Another way to get the best possible value when buying rental real estate is to look for a building that sits on a lot providing extra land that could be developed. You might be able to add onto the building, erect a new home, or even sell part of the land to offset your purchase cost. Before you contemplate such a strategy, however, determine whether you will need a zoning variance to subdivide the land.

Vacation Homes

One of the more pleasurable forms of real estate investment is a vacation home because you can live there up to 14 days a year or 10 percent of the amount of time you rent it, whichever is less (according to the tax code). If you own a home in a desirable location near a beach, lake, ski resort, or tourist attraction, you should be able to rent out the property for at least part of the year. In the best of all worlds, your annual rental income would cover your expenses or even exceed them. That would mean that you could live in the house rent free during your vacations. Unless your property is extremely popular, however, you should not expect to enjoy a positive cash flow.

A vacation home can provide tax benefits if it produces negative cash flow – in other words, costs more than it earns in rent. That's because the tax law allows you to deduct up to $25,000 of business losses from your *adjusted gross income* (AGI), as long as you actively rent and maintain the property. You qualify for the full $25,000 write-off if your AGI is less than $100,000. From $100,000 to $150,000 in income, the tax benefit is phased out. If you earn more than $150,000, you can deduct business losses only against rental income, not against regular income from your job or other investments. In calculating business losses, you can count all your expenses for maintaining the property, including depreciation, painting, yard maintenance, property taxes, insurance, and utility bills. You are also allowed to count any trips you take to inspect or repair the property. If you abuse this right of visitation, the IRS may consider your vacation home a personal, not a rental, property.

If you take out a mortgage to purchase a vacation home, you can deduct your mortgage interest on your tax return. While that deduction may be sizable, it also increases your expenses considerably and makes it more difficult to generate positive cash flow.

When looking for a vacation home to buy as a rental, you should hunt for a property that has already been rented for several seasons. This will earn you a return clientele and give you a realistic indication of the level of rent to expect. If you improve the property, you might even be able to increase the rent somewhat. If you're going to charge a hefty rent, though, the property must be in excellent condition, offer comfortable furnishings, and provide modern appliances that work. You might be able to rent the property yourself with ads in the local newspaper, but if that doesn't work, you will have to hire a rental agent, who might charge as much as 25 percent of the rent you collect.

In the end, you should not purchase a vacation home primarily as an investment that you expect will earn substantial capital appreciation. Instead, aim to generate a positive cash flow and maximize your tax benefits. If you get to live at the home two weeks every year for free, you've got yourself a good deal.

Timeshares

While they are often sold as real estate investments, timeshares are, in fact, not investments at all. When you purchase a timeshare, you own a specific block of time – usually a week – at a particular place – usually a condominium in a resort area. Before you buy, you must be convinced that you like the unit, development and surrounding area so much that you will want to come back year after year on your vacation.

Owners of timeshare units built by developers that are members of the Resort Property Owners Association (P.O. Box 2395, Northbrook, IL 60062; 708-291-0710) can swap their units with other members at properties around the world. However, unless you own a share in a very popular resort at a highly desirable time of year, you may not be able to trade for a place you want to go. If you become ill or an emergency arises in your week for the timeshare, you probably will have to forfeit that week unless you can make a last-minute swap.

The high-pressure salespeople who sell timeshare units usually pitch the excellent resale potential of their developments. Don't believe it. Hundreds of thousands of people can't find buyers because the salespeople direct most potential purchasers to new units. If you still want to buy a timeshare, you will probably get the best deal by purchasing an existing unit at a deep discount.

Be particularly wary of telemarketing firms that sell timeshares. Some of them claim to have extensive lists of sales agents and buyers lining up for their resale units. The more audacious promoters will even charge up to $500 for an "advance listing," promising that you can resell your unit for a quick profit. Some actually offer money-back guarantees.

Timeshare units are not only illiquid; they impose maintenance charges you must pay whether you use the your unit or not. Even those who try to abandon their timeshares meet with little luck. The developer and timeshare owners association pursue them to collect the money due according to the contract.

Nevertheless, if you want to own a timeshare, begin by renting an apartment a few times in the development in which you are interested. If you really like the development and want to return frequently, it might be worth buying into it. However, try to buy into a development backed by a major, well-known corporation – such as Marriott, Disney, or Hilton – rather than some fly-by-night operation. Consider your purchase a way to lock in a long-term price for a vacation. It's unlikely to be an investment that grows in value over time.

To learn more about timeshares from the industry's point of view, contact the American Resort Development Association (1220 L St., N.W., 5th Floor, Washington, DC 20005; 202-371-6700).

Raw Land

Picture the following: You buy a piece of raw land cheaply from owners who have been sitting on it for years, unaware of its true value. Knowing that the area is about to be developed, you sell the acreage to developers and reap huge profits. That's the dream. The reality of investing in raw land is usually quite different.

Most raw land is purchased by developers assembling a site for a housing project, a shopping center, a factory, or another commercial use. The land's value rises once utilities, roads, sewers, and other amenities are installed. The prospect of quick gains usually encourages investment houses to sponsor *raw land*, or *predevelopment, limited partnerships*, but most fail. The combination of high interest rates and a glut of commercial properties in many markets hurt the value of raw land throughout the United States in the 1990s.

Raw land is usually illiquid, meaning that it can be difficult to sell. In addition, unless you rent the land to someone, the property produces no income. Meanwhile, you incur expenses such as maintenance and property taxes. If you borrow to buy the land, you must meet regular interest payments as well. This negative cash flow can drain your budget and makes sense only if you feel sure the land will rise in value soon.

Many factors affect the selling price of land, including the state of the local economy, the direction of interest rates, local zoning and environmental regulations and changing tax laws. Any one of these factors can turn against the owner of raw land. For example, the property may be rezoned to a use with less commercial potential, hurting the land's value. Or the land may be classified as a wetland, making it unsaleable. Or an inspector may find traces of toxic waste from a previous owner that you must clean up before you sell the property. Even if the land is clean, you should determine how difficult it will be to get water, electricity, sewage systems, and roads to the site. Before you buy, know everything about a piece of land, including its present condition and development potential.

In most cases, it has been difficult for raw land values to rise much in the face of increasing property tax burdens, strict zoning enforcement, and slow economic growth. Buying raw land is therefore the most speculative real estate investment. You might hit it big with a combination of luck and inside knowledge, but don't count on it.

Investing in real estate – both in your home and in other investment property – will always hold great appeal for Americans. More people in this country have amassed fortunes in real estate than in any other asset. By buying a home, you not only acquire pride of ownership; you get real value out of your property by using it every day, even if its market value falls. Investment real estate offers potential capital appreciation, income, and tax breaks – as well as headaches.

The era of the 1970s and early 1980s, when almost every piece of real estate appreciated dramatically, has passed, probably forever. To succeed in real estate investment now, you must study the markets carefully and understand the complex financing options and tax laws that cause values to rise and fall. You need to depend less on luck and more on expertise.

[SEVEN]

Investment Strategies for
Every Age Category

The transition from school to the work force can be both exhilarating and frustrating. Once you land a job after graduation, you may feel the thrill of financial independence from your parents for the first time. Yet your starting salary may be far too low to purchase your first home or even rent your own apartment. In addition, you may be loaded with debts accumulated to pay for your education. As you progress through your 30s, your career should become more firmly established, your income and assets should grow, and you should gain total financial independence from your parents. While in your youth, you can do plenty to establish good financial habits. In fact, there's no better time to start!

Investing

Start to assemble a portfolio of stocks, bonds, and mutual funds as early as you can afford to save. Aim to set aside as much as 10 percent of your after-tax income. If you don't have much capital, mutual funds probably make more sense than individual stocks or bonds. Funds require minimum initial investments of only $250 to $1,000 and offer diversification. One easy way to invest in funds is to enroll in an automatic investment program in which a mutual fund group deducts a set amount, such as $100 a month, from your checking account and deposits it in whatever fund you choose. Several fund groups even waive their minimum initial investments if you commit to an automatic investing plan.

Favor stock funds over bond funds because stock funds have much more growth potential over the long haul than bond funds. You might allocate 70 to 80 percent of your savings to equity funds, with a high proportion of that money in aggressive growth, growth, and international funds, which will probably provide the highest long-term returns. Bonds pay regular income, but that is probably not as important in this stage of life as growth of capital. Unless you have a great deal of extra money and time to learn, avoid speculating in futures, options, gold, and collectibles while in your 20s and 30s.

Also, establish a good relationship with a bank. If you can build up enough money in checking and savings accounts to meet minimum requirements, you can save hundreds of dollars in monthly account and per-check fees. In addition, keep an emergency reserve fund in a bank or money-market mutual fund of at least three months' living expenses in case you get laid off, suffer a medical emergency, have a large car repair bill, or incur some other unforeseen expense.

[Your 40s and 50s: The Peak Earning Years of Middle Age]

When you enter your peak earning years, you may join what many call the sandwich generation. At the same time that you support your children, perhaps paying their college tuition bills, your financial and other responsibilities for your parents may grow as well if they are still alive and have not saved enough to live comfortably in retirement. Meanwhile, you have your own expenses to worry about, as well as a need to save for retirement. Many middle-agers short-change themselves by disbursing their assets among their children and parents. The only solution to this dilemma is careful planning and tracking of your personal finances so you can set targets and monitor your progress toward them. If you delay this budgeting process, your retirement years inevitably will suffer.

Investing

If you have already established a substantial portfolio of stocks and equity mutual funds, you might begin to scale back the risk level of your holdings as you move through your 40s and 50s. If 70 percent of your portfolio consisted of aggressive growth or growth stocks when you were in your 20s and 30s, 30 to 50 percent is more appropriate now. You can allocate the rest of your capital to more conservative growth and income investments, such as equity-income, balanced, and convertible mutual funds. Also, increase your bond holdings to about 50 to 70 percent of your portfolio over time, and reinvest the dividends if you don't need the income the bonds generate. If you are in the top tax bracket, consider investing your money in municipal bonds rather than taxable Treasuries or corporates. If you have excess risk capital that you can afford to lose, you might dabble in more speculative arenas, such as options, futures, gold, collectibles, and limited partnerships, but move cautiously.

If you have not saved or invested over the years, do so immediately. Aim to set aside at least 10 percent of your after-tax income – as much as 15 percent, if possible. If your employer offers a salary reduction plan and you have not yet enrolled, do so to the maximum extent possible, particularly if the company matches your contribution. By not saving over the past 20 or more years, you have forgone a tremendous opportunity for which you must now compensate. Your goal is to create a large enough pool of capital to generate the income you need to live well in retirement, which is now only 10 to 25 years away. If you can amass $100,000, that will create an income stream of $5,000 a year if you earn a 5 percent return and $10,000 a year if you manage 10 percent.

Your banking relationships should be well established by now, and you should be maintaining checking, savings, and certificate of deposit (CD) balances high enough to avoid account fees and per-check charges. If you keep money in several banks, consolidate it in one institution to minimize fees. Make sure that your account is insured by the Federal Deposit Insurance Corporation (FDIC).

[Your 60s and Up:
The Retired Years]

If you have planned for retirement most of your working life, the transition into retirement starting in your 60s should be relatively smooth. Ideally, you will have accumulated enough capital through a combination of employee benefits plans and personal investments to produce enough income to live comfortably. You will have developed enough hobbies and other interests aside from your job that you will not feel at a loss about what to do with all the free time that retirement offers. And you will have given thought to your retirement housing options and done some estate planning.

Few people actually get around to mapping out all these aspects of their retirement ahead of time. However, don't think of retirement as lasting a few short years before you die, as earlier generations did. Today, the average life expectancy for someone in good health who retires in his or her early 60s is at least 20 years, and many retirees live into their 90s or even 100s. Therefore, you have many golden years for which to plan. As you enter your preretirement and retirement years, evaluate each aspect of your personal finances so you can enjoy an active and stimulating retirement.

Investing

Once you stop bringing home a salary, you might be tempted to convert your investment portfolio from a broad mix of stocks, bonds, and cash instruments to solely income-oriented bonds. That could be the worst investment move you'll ever make. If you live for another 20 or 30 years, not only will your portfolio have to provide you with current income; it must also protect you against inflation. Someone who retired in the 1950s might have felt totally secure putting all his or her money in long-term bonds yielding about 3 percent. But over the next few decades, the purchasing power of the money would have been devalued considerably by rampaging inflation. Therefore, if you lock yourself into current yields by buying only bonds, your capital will not grow as it most likely will if you own stocks.

So the best investing strategy in retirement is to assemble a conservative mix of stocks, bonds, and cash vehicles that produces enough income to live on but also grows in value over time. This might mean keeping about 80 percent of your assets in cash instruments, like money-market funds, and fixed-income assets, such as Treasury, high-quality corporate, junk and municipal bonds, mortgage-backed securities, and the mutual funds that hold these assets. In assessing which bond fund is best, scrutinize expense ratios; the greater a fund's expenses, the less your yield. Bond funds should have expense ratios of 1.3 percent or less, and preferably less than 1 percent of their assets – a figure you can determine by looking at the cover of the prospectus or asking a fund representative. Also, consider closed-end bond funds, which can offer very attractive yields, particularly if they sell at a discount. Depending on whether yields make it profitable, some of this fixed-income money could be invested in certificates of deposit (CDs).

Invest the remaining 20 percent of your money in stocks or stock mutual funds, which provide an inflation hedge. Most of these stocks and funds should be high yielding so they give you current income, as well as growth. To find safe, high-yielding stocks, search such industries as electric, gas, water and telephone utilities, banking, oil, and insurance. If you would like to have a bit of fun, invest a small portion of your portfolio – perhaps 10 percent – in more speculative growth stocks. Be prepared to lose some or all of this money, and don't invest cash you can't afford to part with. For a more diversified portfolio, buy mutual funds holding mostly high-yielding stocks. Types of funds you might want in your portfolio that offer growth potential and current income include total return, balanced, flexible, equity-income, growth and income, and convertible funds. You can buy such funds in either open-end or closed-end form.

As the value of your portfolio changes over time, keep a proper mix of income and growth components. For example, if the stock market rises sharply, your equity portion may rise significantly beyond 20 percent. Thus, you might consider selling some of the stocks and reinvesting the money in bonds, which will produce more income. If stock prices fall, you might buy stocks at bargain prices with some of the income from your bonds.

Conclusion

As you now understand by having read this *Guide*, the world of investing is clearly complex. While the types of investment decisions you make should be related to your age category, there are still certain universal principles that you should apply no matter how old you are. There is no limit to the amount of knowledge you can gain on the many topics described in this *Guide*. We hope that we have provided you with a framework to understand your investment options and thereby make wise investing decisions. In order to monitor the attractiveness of your various investment options, as the economy and markets change, we encourage you to put this *Guide* into action as you read MONEY Magazine every month. Set your financial goals, establishing a systematic way to invest, and keep on top of developments in your portfolio. With this *Guide* and MONEY Magazine on your side, you can achieve life-long financial security.

Notes